Faith in Search of
Understanding

FAITH IN SEARCH OF UNDERSTANDING:

An Introduction to Theology

Charles Hill

GILL AND MACMILLAN

Published in Ireland by
Gill and Macmillan Ltd
Goldenbridge
Dublin 8
with associated companies in
Auckland, Delhi, Gaborone, Hamburg, Harare,
Hong Kong, Johannesburg, Kuala Lumpur, Lagos, London,
Manzini, Melbourne, Mexico City, Nairobi,
New York, Singapore, Tokyo
© Charles Hill, 1989, 1991
First published 1989 by Collins Dove, Victoria
0 7171 1892 4
Printed in Australia

Nihil Obstat: Rev. Peter J. Kenny D.D.,
                   Diocesan Censor
Imprimatur: Hilton F. Deakin Ph.D.,
                   Vicar General
Date: 22nd August, 1989

The Nihil Obstat and Imprimatur are official declarations
that a book or pamphlet is free of doctrinal or moral error.
No implication is contained therein that those who have
granted the Nihil Obstat and Imprimatur agree with the
contents, opinions or statements expressed. They do not
necessarily signify that the work is approved as basic text
for catechetical instruction.

To
the Catholic Adult Education group
of Penrith–Lower Mountains NSW
for their inspiration and perseverance
in bringing people to a sense of Church

I have written this little work from the viewpoint
of a person trying to raise his mind to contemplate God
and seeking to understand what he believes.

St Anselm of Canterbury, 11th century, introducing
his work on theology, *Faith Seeking Understanding*

So, understand with a view to faith; have faith with a
view to understanding. I will explain in a nutshell how to
take this without arousing controversy: Understand my
word with a view to faith, have faith in God's word with
a view to understanding.

St Augustine, 5th century, Sermon 43 on Isaiah 7:9

CONTENTS

Introduction

Our Fathers (and Mothers) in the faith had little patience with the writing of books to no purpose. The Old Testament sage laments even at that time the ceaseless flow of publication ('Of making many books there is no end': Ecclesiastes 12:12), and the writer of the postscript to John's Gospel recognises the futility of trying to do justice to Jesus in books without number (John 21:25). Both sceptics, however, were not averse to adding to the pile.

Were there available suitable texts introducing adults to the study of theology from a Catholic perspective, this book too could fall under their strictures. The wider theological disciplines, however, have not been as well served in this regard as biblical studies, where a range of 'Introductions' (no elementary text in that science) are available, and where, as well, a Catholic character does not need to be explicit. By contrast, there is a dearth of Introductions to theology, particularly those acknowledging the nuances of Catholicism. The older style Fundamental Theology texts are outdated, more recent ones too difficult (e.g., F. Schüssler Fiorenza's *Foundational Theology*, Crossroad, New York, 1984). Gerald O'Collins's *Fundamental Theology*, Paulist, New York, 1981, suitable if quite challenging, is unfortunately out of print.

Yet the many adults interested in 'doing theology' require some assistance if they come to the study without a sound background (as is often the case). Furthermore, these students proceeding to further theological study could do with introduction to several aspects of theology not normally considered in introductory texts. In addition to the nature, concepts, idioms, divisions, sources of theology and theological processes, an appropriate text should also address the need students have of **some sense of history of the Christian community and its theologising**. Also, along with attention to biblical and liturgical traditions — tradition being a much misunderstood notion among Catholics — there is need to study the **moral tradition** of Christianity if students are later to approach moral theology and moral education with some inkling of morality and moral decision-making.

Hence the justification for this text and its structure. Chapters have been arranged in historical sequence to show the interplay in history of key theological notions. Critical moments have been chosen along a time-line reaching from the Old Testament to contemporary theological movements; other moments could be selected to fill out the picture of the Christian community's theologising.

At the end of each chapter, references are given to some relevant works, and a gentle introduction is made to journal reading. Exercises intended to lend a practical slant to 'doing theology' are also included there.

The reason for adopting in the present text a slant different from some of the works referred to on theology lies in my association over the years with graduate students, who have brought to the study of theology both a richness of experience and also a sense of need. Acknowledgement should also go to my colleagues in Catholic adult education who have read the text and suggested ways of improving its impact on the reader: Marcellin Flynn, Gideon Goosen, Brian Grenier, Brian Lewis, Geoff Plant. As they all exemplify conspicuously St Thomas's motto for the Christian teacher, *contemplata aliis tradere*, I have striven to implement their suggestions; readers will benefit from these, and I too am grateful.

Acknowledgement is made of permission to publish excerpts from other works: to SCM Press, London, *Genesis* by Gerhard Von Rad, 1972; Harvill Press, London, *St John Chrysostom* by Donald Attwater, 1959; Fortress Press, Philadelphia, volume 35 of Luther's *Works*, ed. E. Bachmann, 1960; *The Catholic Biblical Quarterly*, the Pontifical Biblical Commission's *Instruction on the Historical Truth of the Gospels*, 1964; Penguin Books Ltd, Harmondsworth, *Early Christian Writings*, ed. A. Louth, 1987; *The Catholic Herald*, Pope John Paul II's address at Puebla; Charles Scribner's Sons, New York, *Jesus and the Word* by Rudolf Bultmann, 1962. Quotations from the Bible are from the Revised Standard Version, copyright 1952 and 1971 by the division of Christian Education of the National Council of the Churches of Christ in the USA.

Charles Hill
Catholic College of Education Sydney

1

Why

'do theology'?

If I sin, what do I do to thee,
    thou watcher of men?
Why hast thou made me thy mark?
Why have I become a burden to thee?

Job 7.20

Who has inflicted this upon us? Who has made us Jews different
to all other people? Who has allowed us to suffer so terribly up
till now? It is God who has made us as we are, but it will be
God, too, who will raise us up again.

The Diary of Anne Frank

We are supposed to be rational animals — if not always
reasonable. So, puzzling things out is as normal for us as a
dog worrying a bone. Things have to make sense; we must
have (at least in our more reflective moments) an explanation
for apparent contradictions, a reason for what happens, a
basis for decision. 'To be, or not to be', ponders a worried
Hamlet; 'that is the question: whether 'tis nobler in the mind
to suffer the slings and arrows of outrageous fortune, or to
take up arms against a sea of troubles and by opposing end
them'. And people have spent a lot of time since Shakespeare
trying to make sense of Hamlet too.

So theology comes naturally to us — theology as an attempt to make sense of what we believe. Hamlet, of course,
was not theologising about the options open to him — only
using his reason, or perhaps rationalising a soft option.

1

Theology, St Anselm told us in the eleventh century, is '**faith seeking understanding**'; our reasoning is done in the light of faith. Poor Job in Old Testament times put to himself and his friends the age-old question 'Why me?', and tried to solve it in the light of what his faith told him of God and humanity; it was not enough, and so the problem lay unanswered until God's Son in a similar predicament offered us the complete answer. At least Job was *theologising*, whereas the advice of Aristotle a little later, 'Those who wish to succeed must ask the right preliminary questions', is only a *philosopher's* wisdom or experience. No faith needed to ask questions — that's only being rational; it's when we subject our beliefs to questioning that we are theologising.

Hamlet, if philosopher rather than theologian, nevertheless highlights the fact that we can often do with prompting to bring our brains to bear on our beliefs. Trouble, suffering, persecution, the world's ills — such things start us thinking, trying to reconcile what we experience with what we believe. Which is why a lot of theology has to do with suffering and evil. Job in his generation and Anne Frank in hers, the Babylonian captivity then and the Holocaust and Hiroshima now: how do we reconcile it all with a loving God? Many cannot, and abandon reason or God in the process. 'Doing theology' is not as simple as solving an equation; Job's friends certainly had their equation wrong.

But **the object of theology** is not just the dark side of life; it is all of life, all that God has shared with us, and himself too — whatever our faith bears on. For Malcolm Muggeridge, the life and work of Mother Teresa of Calcutta was 'something beautiful for God'. It not only made an impression on him, it brought him to belief. 'For me, Mother Teresa of Calcutta embodies Christian love in action. Her face shines with the love of Christ on which her whole life is centred, and her words carry that message to a world that never needed it so much'.

My own impression of Mother Teresa, for what it is worth, was of someone who is conspicuously short on theologising, almost fundamentalist in her acceptance of a gospel others of us worry over. I heard her say this: 'I remember one day they brought a man half of whose body was eaten up with cancer. He was so smelly that nobody could stand with him. I happened to be in the house with him and I started washing him. And he said to me, "Why are you doing this?" And I said to him what Jesus said. He was a Hindu man and I told

2

him what Jesus had said. And I said, "I really believe I am touching his body in you". And then he said, "Glory to Jesus Christ through you!" And I said, "No, but glory to Jesus Christ through you, because you are sharing in his passion".' Such literalism comes as a shock to a professional theologian, suggesting the limits of mere theology.

A reminder here that **theology is not all books and words**. People have expressed their faith and the questions it raises for them in other forms. Whereas conventional painters have represented the Christian mysteries in a soothing manner, to study a Dali or Chagall or El Greco is to set us wondering what meaning the artist found in the biblical text. The comfortable crucifixions of Old Masters contrast starkly with the tortured Cristo of a Third World artist painting out of a situation of oppression and deprivation that has made him read the Gospels differently. The melodrama of a medieval *Stabat Mater* or *Dies Irae* suggests an interpretation of the scriptural text that biblical scholars today would deny was the purpose of the evangelists, who were more interested in austere dogmatic truth than in heart-rending pathos. All these creative artists have in their own way, rightly or wrongly, theologised about their beliefs before putting paint to canvas or music to notation.

So **'doing theology'** is natural for us believers, as reasoning is for all human beings. Perhaps like Hamlet we can think too much, and like Mother Teresa we should instead move directly from faith to action. But there will be times — dark times as well as luminous ones — when our faith will seek understanding, and the habit that theology is will stand us in good stead. It is a habit to be developed; the following pages suggest how this can be done and in fact has been done by believers down the ages.

The world needs theologians. Yes, this absurd little earth, where a billion humans fall asleep hungry, this glorious globe that was freed from slavery by the crucifixion of its God, this paradoxical planet that nurtures love and hate, despair and hope, skepticism and faith, tears and smiles, wine and blood, this creation of divine love where men and women die for one another and kill one another — this world desperately needs theologians.

Why? To interpret this bittersweet experience, this bloody mess, to ask what it's all about. And precisely this is the theologian's task: struggling, agonizing to understand and express. It is your privilege and your burden to search out *where* God has spoken, where God speaks: from the burning bush in

3

Midian to the gas ovens in Auschwitz, from the word that was creation to the Word that was made flesh, from the church gathered in council to the skin-and-bones dying that defecate at Calcutta's curbstones, from the Book that somehow reveals the heart of God to the trace of God on the face of humanity.

W. Burghardt, 'This world desperately needs theologians', *Catholic Mind* 79 (March 1981) 34

Some relevant reading

Carmody, J. and Carmody, D., *Contemporary Catholic Theology*, Harper and Row, San Francisco, 1985.

Fisher, K. and Hart, T., *Christian Foundations. An Introduction to Faith in Our Time*, Paulist, New York, 1986.

Monk, R. and Stamey, J., *Exploring Christianity*, Prentice Hall, Englewood Cliffs, 1984.

Shelly, B., *Church History in Plain Language*, Word Books, Waco, 1982.

Exercises in theology

(1) We often find ourselves puzzling over life's injustices, pleasant surprises, and the twists and turns of fate. Do we acknowledge that this can involve theologising as we endeavour to reconcile daily events with our beliefs?

(2) We see and hear much theology — good and bad — in the Old Masters and modern composers and artists. Choose a hymn, a painting, or piece of writing that involves expression of belief, and trace the author's attempt to bring understanding to faith.

(3) At what age do children begin to ponder their faith, to make sense of what they (or the faith community) believe — in other words, to theologise? Have you thought about the place of theology in religious education? (You may care to glance ahead to Chapter 13).

2

Theology

in the

making:

Old Testament creeds

For Christian theologians — that is, all of us who think about our Christian beliefs — the Old Testament has always been an important document of religious history. It has provided us with details of the Jewish people's religious practices and institutions, their cult (or worship) and festivals, and the office bearers in this cult. And we see this religious history linked with ours because we comprehend the dimensions of the mystery, the vast sacred reality, that is Christ.

But as we have come to understand the Old Testament better, it has been seen not simply to present a history of **religion** — something man-made, a product of the Jews themselves, unlike **faith**, that springs from God's initiative — but to represent a **theological** statement, an attempt to make sense of their beliefs in the light of their experiences as a people. Faith, in Old Testament terms, has been described as 'saying Amen to God', the roots of that word 'Amen' stating all there is to be said of God's truth and dependability. For Job, however, saying Amen to God amidst all his vicissitudes was not enough; he set about theologising frantically to reconcile faith and daily reality — **faith seeking understanding**, in that later definition of theology. And he was joined in

5

this theological endeavour by other Old Testament figures and composers.

Our sharper appreciation of **the Old Testament as theology** comes from the science of biblical criticism. (Criticism here, as in other areas of literary study, carries its original neutral sense of 'judgement, evaluation'; see Chapter 8 for further detail.) Earlier this century the great German scholar Gerhard Von Rad produced his monumental studies on the opening six books of the Bible. Von Rad not only traced the literary movement in this six-fold work running from the patriarchs in Genesis to the people's settlement in the land in Joshua; he also highlighted the theological activity of the various composers of the text. In this he was accepting the evidence of scholars from the time of the priest Richard Simon in the seventeenth century for a looser understanding of authorship of the Torah by Moses; the evidence suggests that many hands have been at work in our present text, resulting in more than one creation story, more than one flood story, more than one giving of the Commandments, etc.

Going further, Von Rad pointed to the antiquity of certain passages in the text, stating that they preserve a pithy statement of basic beliefs of people at the time of composition. These Von Rad styled 'cultic credos' because they were recited in liturgical settings like our creeds. One such is embedded in the text of Deuteronomy at the point where the composers are reporting Moses' directions for presentation of first fruits by the worshipper, who is at that moment to recite his belief in the following formula (26:5–9):

> A wandering Aramean was my father; and he went down into Egypt and sojourned there, few in number; and there he became a nation, great, mighty, and populous. And the Egyptians treated us harshly, and afflicted us, and laid upon us hard bondage. Then we cried to the Lord the God of our fathers, and the Lord heard our voice, and saw our affliction, our toil, and our oppression; and the Lord brought us out of Egypt with a mighty hand and an outstretched arm, with great terror, with signs and wonders; and he brought us into this place and gave us this land, a land flowing with milk and honey.

We may wonder why, at the moment of offering gifts, a narrative is recited of God's care for his people — his choice of them in the patriarchs (in this case Jacob, the wandering Aramean), his deliverance of them from slavery through the marvels of the Exodus, his conduct of them into the Land. And yet, on reflection, we recall that our creeds tell of God's actions (through Jesus, in the Spirit) for the Church; we might think also of the wording of Eucharistic prayers. Like our creeds this cultic credo in Deuteronomy springs from theological reflection on a people's experience of their God to focus on what is basic; it is not a list of divine attributes but a series of actions that comes into focus as central to faith.

In his famous commentary on Genesis Von Rad comments on the credo:

> There can be no doubt that this is how one really spoke in ancient times, and we can see within the cultic framework it was customary, among other things, to recite a short form of the sacred history as a confession. For what the man here utters is a kind of credo, not a personal prayer of thanksgiving. There is no divinely addressed Thou; the whole thing is completely and strikingly divested of every personal note. The speaker recapitulates the great, sacred facts that constitute the community. He abstains from all individual concerns and in this moment identifies himself completely with the community; that is, he makes a confession of faith.
> A similar creedal summation of the sacred history occurs in Deut. 6.20–24. The text, which is now completely imbedded in the great parenetic context, is easily recognisable as having been originally independent, both with regard to form and content.
> We may add still a third example, the speech of Joshua before the assembly at Shechem. It is somewhat more extensive because of a few embellishments, but there can be no doubt that basically this historical review is not a distinct literary creation. Here too, apparently, an essentially fixed form is used, a form with which one can take only minor liberties.
> The old cultic traditions in particular were previously unthinkable outside the sacred framework. Only in the course of the cultic act could one meet and experience them. These sacred traditions were not some kind of ornamental addition to the cult; rather, they were its inmost nerve, by which it lived and from which proceeded the content and form of the festivals.

The significant features and processes that Von Rad discerns in these cultic credos in Deuteronomy 6 and 26 and Joshua 24 mark the passages out from mere Bible stories (where the emphasis falls more on spectacular incident than on theological reflection). His interest falls on 'facts', 'experience', 'sacred history', 'traditions', 'community', 'confession of faith', 'credo', 'cult', 'festivals'. He then goes on to talk of

7

the theological shaping at the hands of the great composers, who took such primitive compositions and welded them into our continuous text, from which emerges the picture of a God choosing and delivering a people of his own — the central theological message of the Old Testament. In this view the Old Testament becomes much more than a simple history of Israel's religious practices and institutions; it is primarily **the work of sophisticated theologians** shaping inherited material as they wrestle with the interrelationship of their beliefs: first, faith in the God who acts, and theological reflection on this faith; only of secondary importance are the religious practices devised ('commanded', in the wording of the present text) to express that faith.

For our study of the nature of theology, these cultic credos of the Old Testament can exemplify some of the components of the theological process. The process presumes and occurs within the **relationship** between **God** and the **individual** — in Deuteronomy 26 the worshipper presenting first fruits in temple or shrine — but also within the relationship between God and the **community**/people/church, who have adopted these creeds for themselves.

At the roots of that relationship, the individual/community has undergone significant **experience(s)**; in this case, the People of Israel recall their choice or election by Yahweh, his deliverance of them in the Exodus, and their entry into the land of promise — a pattern that is basic to all Old Testament credal statements. In the course of time this religious experience has been mulled over and *discerned* as authentic, *interpreted* for the **revelation** about God and his designs that it betokens, *expressed in word and eventually in writing*, and committed to *memory* (see the diagram on p. 9).

The response of the community and the individual to this experience, which is both a **saving** and a revelatory experience, is a response of faith; this **faith** is **confessed** in cultic credos, like these Deuteronomic ones, and as well as *confession* it involves also *commitment* to this 'God who acts' and *confidence* in him.

The importance of this saving, revelatory experience and the depth of the faith response lead to repeated recital of the experience, held in the community's collective **memory**, and then to its faithful transmission or **tradition** to later generations (orally first, and then in writing). The experience, besides its response in a people's **faith**, also evokes a **religious** expression in the form of cultic **celebration**, especially

8

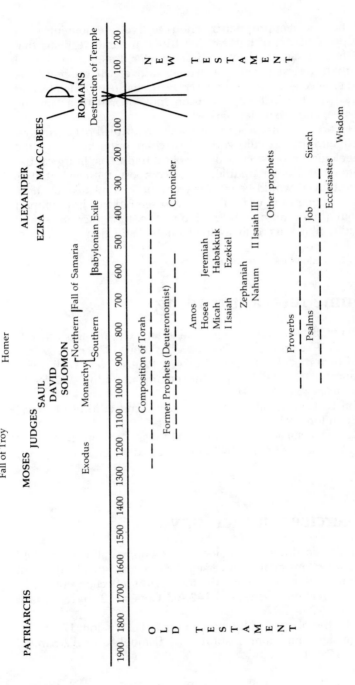

Composition of the Bible: A time-line of key figures, events, authors

at the time of appropriate religious **festivals** or moments such as presentation of harvest first fruits. In Israel festivals that were originally agricultural in character thus became linked with historical events, such as Passover, to celebrate the experience — hence the references in that feast to lambs and yeast, as the historical occasion took over both a lambing festival and the barley harvest.

Hence, in this process of tradition, **Bible**/book/scripture/ text and **liturgy**/cult/worship play an important role; the theological process considers biblical traditions, liturgical traditions and other traditions that compose the community's tradition. It would be (and is commonly) a mistake to think only of one form of tradition, or to see Bible or liturgy apart from (other forms of) tradition. The term 'scripture and tradition' is thus really an inadequate distinction.

Some relevant reading

Childs, B., 'Introduction to the Pentateuch', in *Introduction to the OT as Scripture*, SCM Press, London, 1979, pp. 109–35.

O'Collins, G., *Fundamental Theology*, Paulist, New York, 1981.

Thornhill, J., 'Is religion the enemy of faith?' *Theological Studies* 45 (1984) 254–74.

Von Rad, G., *Studies in Deuteronomy*, 2nd edn, SCM Press, London, 1953.

——, *Deuteronomy*, 2nd edn, SCM Press, London, 1966.

——, *Genesis*, 9th edn, SCM Press, London, 1972.

Exercises in theology

(1) To see different theological viewpoints at work in Old Testament material, read versions of the same story by different composers, and compare the theological reflection involved:
  (a) creation: Genesis 1:1–2:4a; Genesis 2:4b–25; Sirach 16:26–17:17;
  (b) the plagues in Egypt: Exodus 7–11; Wisdom 17–18;
  (c) kingship as an institution: 1 Samuel 8:4–22; 2 Samuel 7:4–17.

(2) Compare Christian creeds (e.g. Apostles Creed, Nicene–Constantinopolitan Creed) for their differences one to the other in theological viewpoint and their degree of similarity to Old Testament creeds (see Appendix).

(3) Examine the wording of our Eucharistic prayers for the kinds of theological reflection involved. Do they resemble Old Testament cultic credos?

(4) 'I get nothing out of Sunday Mass' is a comment heard occasionally, from young people in particular. Is there implicit in this complaint a legitimate desire for religious experience that lies at the basis of faith, or is it a reflection of mere immaturity? To what extent should the liturgy transmit the community's foundational experiences and allow us to share in them personally?

3

Confessing faith

in

Jesus:

the letters of Paul

Biblical criticism, which has highlighted the theological activity that has gone into the apparently uncomplicated process of composition of Old Testament texts, has also brought to light the theologising practised by the evangelists and other New Testament authors. Hence we no longer see biblical inspiration as some kind of mechanical 'zapping' that deprived biblical authors of their own initiative. Instead, we have come to recognise the **individual theological contributions of the New Testament writers**, while acknowledging as well the unwritten traditions about Jesus, handed on by the early Christian communities, that underlay the later written compositions. The Jesus of Matthew and the Jesus of John both owe something to these traditions, and something to Matthew's and John's own reflection and accents — their theologising, in other words.

As with Old Testament texts, therefore, so with the New Testament Gospels and letters/epistles we observe the same components of the theological process: a **relationship** with God ('testament' being an unfortunate Latin term for relationship) arising from religious **experience** that offers **revelation** and prompts a response of **faith** that is confessed, the community's **memory** at work, **tradition**/transmission of the experience, and its cultic **celebration**. So too with the New Testament; despite the deceptively uniform and uncomplicated appearance of our modern texts in translation, we need to be aware of the processes that have gone to produce them. As 'Moses' represents a vast number of contributors to the Torah in the hundreds of years of its composition, so behind Matthew stand witnesses and contributors to the story of Jesus, the New Torah.

The Gospels provide an obvious example of the lengthy and manifold process of composition underlying our texts. The teaching Church has discouraged us from taking a fundamentalist view of Gospel composition; the modern media of communication, with their immediate and exact replay of word and incident, bear little resemblance to the gradual movement from event to written record that characterised ancient oriental cultures. At each stage of Gospel tradition about Jesus, over many decades, **theologising** has gone on about his significance, notably but not exclusively by the evangelist — and perhaps even by some later editor of a Gospel.

The letters of Paul, who met his death before the Roman destruction of Jerusalem in AD 70, are generally conceded to have been written closer to the time of Jesus than the Gospels, probably by several decades. They come more or less directly from Paul without intermediate stages of transmission, and so the process of composition of these letters is less complicated than in the case of the Gospels. But they are nonetheless theological; Paul stands with the evangelists as **a great New Testament theologian**, and at periods in Christian history he has been read more avidly than the Gospels.

A particularly deliberate statement of the Christian message by Paul occurs at 1 Corinthians 15:1–5:

1 Now, I remind you, brethren, in what terms I preached to you
   the Gospel,
      which you received,
      in which you stand,
2   by which you are saved,
   if you hold it — unless you believed in vain.
3 For I delivered to you as of first importance what I also received,
     that Christ died for our sins
        in accordance with the Scriptures,
4   that he was buried,
     that he was raised on the third day
        in accordance with the Scriptures,
5   that he appeared (to Cephas, then to the Twelve, . . .).

The deliberateness of Paul's tone, the repetitive rhythm of vv. 1–2, the technical character of the vocabulary of catechesis — 'delivered . . . received' — in v. 3, and especially the carefully balanced structure of vv. 3–5 all reinforce Paul's insistence that the message is 'of first importance'. What he is transmitting here, in the form it was transmitted to him, is **the basic Christian kerygma** or proclamation about Jesus. It takes a brief, clear and logically established shape:

JESUS DIED — as the Scriptures forecast — and his burial proves it;
JESUS ROSE — as the Scriptures forecast — and his appearances prove it.

In this version of Paul's, the Christian kerygma, what is 'of first importance' about Jesus, is reduced to the Paschal Mystery, the great sacred reality that Christ's new Passover is; even if all else is to be forgotten, this must be retained. Paul from his own formation and reflection came to the conclusion that this, in the smallest possible nutshell, is the New Testament theology about Jesus, its **Christology**: Jesus died . . . Jesus rose. To us it seems extremely bare; not a shred of the Ministry, not even the Supper.

Yet, though the Gospels may seem to be much more elaborate in their theology of Jesus, they too can be reduced to a brief structural basis on which all four are constructed (and which is represented elsewhere in the New Testament in the 'mini-gospels'):

• PREPARATION FOR JESUS' MINISTRY (Baptism, Temptations);
• JESUS' MINISTRY
• THE PASCHAL MYSTERY.

No birth stories here, no particular parables or miracles — instead a basic pattern leading to that Paschal Mystery of Paul's ('Jesus died . . . Jesus rose'). Biblical criticism has long recognised that a Gospel is accurately seen as 'a Passion narrative with an introduction'; so fundamental to all the Gospels is this unique long narrative. That pattern is what the evangelists inherited from the early Christian community and were powerless to alter; 'Easter ahead of Christmas, if a choice has to be made', is the message Paul also receives and transmits.

The **theology** about Jesus — the Christology — as well as a total theology of God's action in Jesus is clear: central to it is the new Pasch, passion–death–resurrection–exaltation. The Jesus of Bethlehem, Nazareth, Mount of the Beatitudes is secondary. Not that we are surprised: the Old Testament and its central Passover–deliverance–relationship pattern had already sketched out the mystery of Christ in the same terms.

So when Paul at 1 Corinthians 15 formally rehearses his basic teaching, he is inventing no new formula but transmitting the earliest community's proclamation; his theology squares with theirs, and the Gospels and mini-gospels confirm its validity. It rested on their **experience** of the Christ event, as Paul's own electrifying Damascus experience (reported three times in the New Testament) reinforced it for him. It **revealed** clearly for them the God who acts — in Jesus now, as always in the mystery of Christ, and eminently through death and resurrection. It was retained in their **memory**, to be **transmitted** through an early missioner or later through more elaborate Gospels, reaching **biblical** form. It was **celebrated** in **cult**, eminently in the Eucharist; its principal **festival** was a Paschal one.

Paul's journey as a believer and a theologian resembles our own, living as we do at some remove from the life of Jesus. Like him we have to be inserted into the foundational experiences of the Christian community; he was not even born into this community of faith. He was not an eye witness of the ministry of Jesus, reports nothing of it before the Supper in his letters, and admits seeking details of it only from Peter (Galatians 1). He depended on others, agents of tradition, for learning what was 'of first importance' about Jesus. And yet his letters are all about the significance of Jesus, the result of his theologising on these basic beliefs. Admittedly his Damascus experience left an indelible impression on him of his encounter with the Risen Lord. The implication is that every Christian believer, theologian and missionary must in some way come into contact with this foundational experience of the Christian community and share in it personally.

Some relevant reading

Barclay, W., *The Gospels and Acts* I, (2nd edn), SCM Press, London, 1976.

Fitzmyer, J. A., 'Jesus in the early Church through the eyes of Luke–Acts', *Scripture Bulletin* 27 (1987) 26–35.

Jeremias, J., *The Eucharistic Words of Jesus*, (3rd edn), SCM Press, London, 1966.

McArthur, H. (ed.), *In Search of the Historical Jesus*, SPCK, London, 1970.

Mackey, J., *Jesus, the Man and the Myth*, SCM Press, London, 1979.

Pontifical Biblical Commission, *Instruction on the Historical Truth of the Gospels*, Rome, 1964.

Vatican II, *Dogmatic Constitution on Divine Revelation*, Rome, 1965.

Exercises in theology

(1) Read the Pontifical Biblical Commission's *Instruction on the Historical Truth of the Gospels*, and note especially the three stages in the composition of the gospels. Does the *Instruction* suggest theological activity by contributors at the various stages (see Appendix for text)?

(2) In the Acts of the Apostles brief synopses of Jesus' life, or 'mini-gospels', can be detected: 1:21–22; 2:22–24; 10:36–43. Others can be found elsewhere in the New Testament. What is common to them all? In what way do they differ? What theology/theologies emerge from them?

(3) Read the accounts of Paul's Damascus experience in Galatians 1 and Acts 9 and 22. How did it supply for his not being himself an eye witness of the community's foundational experiences? Has it anything to say about all Christians' dependence on these experiences?

4

Theologising in the course of Christian tradition: the Fathers

God's great actions in history have continued to evoke the response of faith in believers since the time of the people of the Old and New Testaments who experienced them directly. This is especially true of God's action *par excellence* in Jesus, and particularly the Paschal Mystery, which is constitutive of the community of believers in Christ — the Christians. For later ages the experience of these great events is no longer direct but to some extent vicarious or relayed — 'dependent' rather than 'foundational', as some would say.

But the processes of **tradition** that ensure transmission of the experience — **biblical** tradition, **liturgical** tradition, **catechetical** tradition, etc. — guarantee that, even if dependent, the experience is nonetheless revelatory and saving for believers in later ages, from earliest times to our own. The community's memory of the experience, its transmission and re-enactment still arouse our faith, which we confess as we celebrate the foundational experience. Is not the same true of Anzac Day in Australia and New Zealand, Independence

Day in the United States of America, and so on in other countries, when people celebrate events constitutive of nationhood that have been passed on to successive generations?

And where there is faith in God's action, even if past, there is continuing reflection, or **theologising**. Hence, in times following the completion of the New Testament, Christians pondered more deeply (even than the evangelists and Paul) God's action in Jesus. In the centuries immediately after the Apostolic age, despite persecution and the Church's struggle for survival, Christian thinkers developed a theology — in fact, **various schools of theology**, depending on differences of geography (East and West), culture, language, philosophy, etc.

These early Christian efforts at developing theology, under pressure from external threat, concentrated largely on the nature of the Church, the Incarnation and person of Jesus, the Trinity, and the true Scriptures. Even while on his way to martyrdom in the amphitheatre in Rome at the turn of the first century, Ignatius, bishop of Antioch, does his bit to correct errors in Christology in writing to one of the churches, Smyrna, visited en route:

> You hold the firmest convictions about our Lord; believing Him to be truly of David's line in His manhood, yet Son of God by the Divine will and power, truly born of a Virgin; baptized by John for His fulfilling of all righteousness; and in the days of Pontius Pilate and Herod the Tetrarch truly pierced by nails in His human flesh (a Fruit imparting life to us from His most blessed Passion), so that by His resurrection He might set up a beacon for all time to call together His saints and believers, whether Jews or Gentiles, in the one body of His Church.
>
> All this He submitted to for our sakes, that salvation might be ours. And suffer He did, verily and indeed; just as He did verily and indeed raise Himself again. His Passion was no unreal illusion, as some sceptics aver who are all unreality themselves. The fate of those wretches will match their belief, for one day they will similarly become phantoms without substance themselves.
>
> For my own part, I know and believe that He was in actual human flesh, even after His resurrection. When He appeared to Peter and his companions, He said to them, 'Take hold of me; touch me, and see that I am no bodiless phantom'.
>
> (*Early Christian Writings*, p. 101)

With the Edict of Toleration and the Emperor Constantine's conversion early in the fourth century, the challenge for the

Church shifted from self-defence to self-definition. The period of the Councils begins, and peace permits **a golden age of theologising** by the great spokesmen, bishops and scholars, whom we call the Fathers of the Church. This patristic theology flourished particularly in the more intellectually fertile, Eastern half of the Empire ruled from Constantinople. Like the Empire, Christendom in those centuries did not recognise only one Roman centre, but looked also to the more ancient patriarchates of Jerusalem, Alexandria, Antioch and Constantinople (see chart).

External tranquillity and absence of persecution allowed domestic rivalries to develop, especially between the two **theological schools** of Alexandria and Antioch, the former Jewish in origin and speculative in its thinking, the latter more pedestrian and pragmatic. These attitudes and antipathies led to quite different approaches to Christology and (consequently) the Scriptures — different theologies, in other words. Their rivalry and theological differences explain the see-sawing of the conciliar debate in the fourth-fifth centuries, council members from one school being unsympathetic to positions held by the other (see map).

One of the greatest of the Greek/Eastern **Fathers of the Church**, St John Chrysostom, preacher of Antioch and later patriarch of Constantinople at the close of the fourth century, reflects his school's preference for the literal (as opposed to the allegorical) sense of Scripture, stemming from an accent on the humanity (less so the divinity) of Jesus. A particular notion of his, to do both with the Scriptures and the correlative doctrine of Incarnation, is God's 'considerateness' (*synkatabasis*) for human limitations in delivering his Word to mankind. Whatever of his relatively uncritical commentary on the biblical text (through lack of linguistic and other skills) we now enjoy, this great pastor develops his theology within scriptural homilies and thus brings his congregation into touch with foundational experiences — something later theology was not always careful to do:

> Do you see the Lord's thoughtful love for man? How he creates and deals with all things in such a way that his own creatures may not just be saved but also regaled with ineffable riches? For this reason he bestowed on us free will, and implanted in our nature and our conscience the knowledge of wickedness and virtue; he allowed the devil to exist, and threatened us with hell so that we should never experience it but reach the kingdom. Why are you

19

surprised that he treats all these things on that basis, and a lot more besides? He who belongs in the bosom of the Father did not decline to take the form of a slave, and submit to all the other limitations of the human condition, to take life of a woman, be born of a virgin, to spend nine months in the womb and take on swaddling clothes, to be known as the son of Joseph, Mary's husband, to grow up gradually, be circumcised, offer sacrifice, to hunger and thirst and feel weariness, and finally to suffer death, and not just death but the kind of death thought most shameful, I mean on a cross — and all this he accepted for you and for your salvation, the Creator of all, the unchanging one, the one who brings all things from nothingness into being, he who surveys the world and makes it tremble, the brightness of whose glory those incorporeal powers the Cherubim cannot gaze upon but hide their faces with the sweep of their wings, leaving the marvel for us to see, he whom angels, archangels and myriad myriads for all eternity acclaim — he it is who, for our sake and for our salvation, did not decline to become man, and marked out for us the ideal way of life, transmitting to us a clear enough teaching by the example of his own life lived in the very human condition he had assumed.

Homily 23 on *Genesis*

Chrysostom preserves both his natural Eastern respect for divine transcendence and, at the same time, thanks to his attention to the text of Scripture, an attachment to the humanity of Jesus, divine immanence. It is an admirable theological balance, again not always achieved by later theologians, who in recent years, owing to their unfamiliarity with the original languages and shifts in fashion, have tended to neglect these great centuries of Christian tradition represented by the Fathers. In an earlier age, on the other hand, a theologian of the eminence of John Henry Newman could claim (perhaps even excessively):

I follow the Fathers, not as thinking that on such a subject they have the weight they possess in the instance of doctrines or ordinances. When they speak of doctrines, they speak of them as being universally held. They are witnesses to the fact of these doctrines having been received, not here or there, but everywhere. We receive these doctrines which they thus teach, not merely because they teach them, but because they bear witness that all Christians everywhere then held them.

20

Principal periods of patristic writing

I The first three centuries AD

A. PRIMITIVE COMPOSITIONS AND APOSTOLIC FATHERS

Roman persecutions *64* ↓	Apostles Creed Didache (Teaching of the Twelve Apostles)	Clement of Rome Ignatius of Antioch Polycarp of Smyrna Papias The Shepherd of Hermas

B. APOLOGISTS AND CONTROVERSIALISTS

Martyrdom of Justin *c. 163*	Justin Martyr Tatian Irenaeus of Lyons

C. EARLY THEOLOGIANS AND CATECHISTS

	East	**West**	
Roman Empire divided *East–West 293*	Clement of Alexandria Origen Dionysius of Alexandria	Tertullian) Cyprian) Lactantius) Hippolytus	*Africa* *Rome*

II The golden age: fourth and fifth centuries AD

	East		**West**
Edict of Toleration 313	School of Alexandria	School of Antioch	Hilary of Poitiers
Conversion of Constantine	Athanasius	Theodore of Mopsuestia	Ambrose
Council of Nicea 325	'The Cappadocians'	John Chrysostom	Jerome
Barbarians in Europe	Basil	Eusebius of Caesarea	Augustine
Council of Constantine 381	Gregory of Nyssa		Paulinus of Nola
Council of Ephesus 431	Gregory of Nazianzen		Pope Leo the Great
Council of Chalcedon 451	Cyril of Alexandria		
Vandals in Africa 429			

III Close of the patristic age: late-fifth to eighth centuries AD

	East	**West**
Last Roman Emperor 476	Dionysius the Areopagite	Benedict
Birth of Mohammed 570	John Climacus	Pope Gregory the Great (+604)
Augustine sent to England 597	John Damascene (+749)	Isidore of Seville (+636)
		Bede the Venerable (+735)

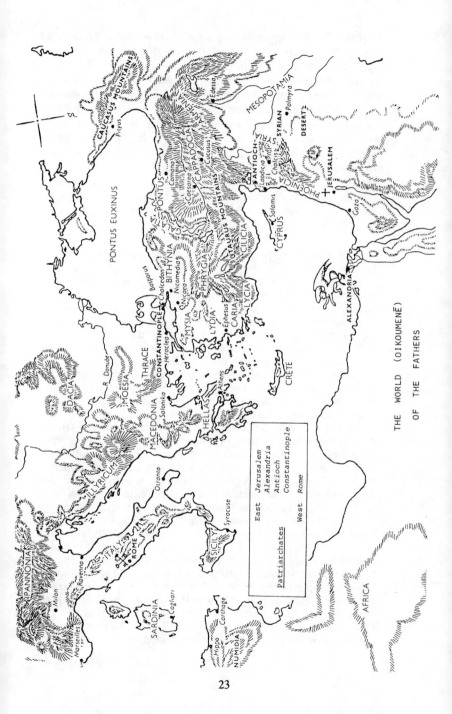

THE WORLD (OIKOUMENĒ)

OF THE FATHERS

Patriarchates

East Jerusalem
      Alexandria
      Antioch
      Constantinople

West Rome

23

Newman thus recognises the significance of the Fathers as vital agents in the process of **doctrinal tradition**, complementing the biblical tradition on which they reflect. (One may question the unanimity he finds in them when one sees, for example, the polemic between Alexandria and Chrysostom's Antioch.) They are important milestones, too, along the line of **moral tradition** in the Christian community. In the passage above, Chrysostom sees the exemplary value of the Incarnation for us, and his homilies are all directed to the lives of his congregation — overly moralistic, in fact, as we shall see in Chapter 10, and not a little *sexist*. He is on firmer ground in dogmatic areas, as for example when bringing out the incarnational character of the Scriptures, again by recourse to his notion of divine considerateness:

Do you see how the Lord, in showing considerateness for human limitations, does everything of set purpose to reveal his own loving kindness? Don't be taken aback, dearly beloved, by the extent of his considerateness; remember instead how in the case of the patriarch Abraham, when he was sitting under the oak tree, he came as a guest to the good man in the form of a man in the company of angels, foreshadowing ahead of time from the beginning that he would one day take human form, and thus free all human nature from the tyranny of the devil and lead them to salvation. In Old Testament times, however, since it was the beginning and a period of preparation, he appeared to each of these men in the form of a vision, as he told them through inspired authors, 'I have multiplied visions, and have taken various forms in the writings of the inspired authors.' But when he deigned to take the form of a slave, and to submit to the little we have to offer, it was not in vision, nor did he take on our flesh in appearance only, but in reality. Accordingly he chose to pass through all our experiences — to be born of a woman, be a babe in arms, be wrapped in swaddling clothes, be fed at the breast, and undergo all other things so that the truth of the divine plan might be confirmed and the mouths of heretics might be stopped. Likewise he sleeps in a boat, travels long journeys, gets tired, and endures all other human distress in order that by means of all he had done he might be able to convince everyone. Likewise he faces a trial, is crucified, endures death of the most ignominious kind, and is placed in a tomb, so that all of this may make clear the pattern of the divine plan. You see, if he had not in reality taken on himself our human flesh, neither would he have been crucified, dead, buried, nor risen again. But if he had not risen, all talk of the divine plan would be contradicted.

(Homily 58 on *Genesis*)

Some relevant reading

Congar, Y., *A History of Theology*, Doubleday, New York, 1968.

Hill, C., 'St John Chrysostom and the Incarnation of the Word in Scripture', *Compass Theology Review*, 14 (1980, Spring) 34–38.

Kelly, J. N. D., *Early Christian Doctrines*, (5th edn), Harper and Row, London, 1978.

Louth, A. (ed.), *Early Christian Writings*, (rev. edn), Penguin, Harmondsworth, 1987.

O'Collins, G., *Fundamental Theology*, Paulist, New York, 1981.

Quasten, J., *Patrology*, 3 vols, Newman, Westminster Md, 1950–60.

Quasten, J. and Di Berardino, A. *Patrology*, vol. 4, Christian Classics, Westminster Md, 1986.

Exercises in theology

(1) Australian historian Manning Clark has said: 'There was no such person as Ned Kelly [a famous bushranger in the early days, later a folk hero]. Indeed, there is no such thing as a human being, in some ways. There is only what he thinks of himself at different periods of time and what other people think of him at different periods of time'. Has this statement about a historical figure any bearing on the degree of dependence we have on Christian tradition for our knowledge of Jesus?

(2) Leaf through a copy of the documents of Vatican II and look at the footnoting of council statements from the early Fathers. What is the purpose of rooting current statement in earlier positions? What does it say of the theological value of these patristic spokesmen?

(3) A great modern theologian, Henri De Lubac, has said of the Fathers: 'I seek only to understand them, and listen to what they have to tell us, since they are our Fathers in the Faith and since they received from the Church of their time the means to nourish the Church of our times as well.' What nourishment for the Church of our times do Ignatius and Chrysostom offer in the passages quoted above?

5

Transmitting the experience within the Church: the Councils

In those first critical centuries following compilation of the Christian Scriptures, the great preachers, writers and teachers whom we call Fathers of the Church served as authentic transmitters of the foundational experiences recorded there. In East and West they pondered them, sought to bring greater understanding to their belief in them — in short, **theologised** about them. Particularly in the troubled times of persecution, these theologians (usually with pastoral responsibilities for the flock) nourished the Church of their time with what they had received and developed from earlier times. As the World Council of Churches said in the statement of its Faith and Order Commission in 1963 at Montreal, '**tradition** taken in this sense is actualised in the preaching of the Word, in the administration of the sacraments and worship, in Christian teaching and theology, and in mission and witness to Christ by the lives of the members of the Church'. In some cases these Fathers also attested to their beliefs by dying for them.

With the easier climate of imperial peace throughout the civilised world, Church members had relative leisure for the work of self-definition through clarification of authentic statement and discernment of error. Those with responsibility for teaching in the Church — the magisterium — now had the opportunity to exercise it; this included both bishops and other theologians, though in the patristic age the great spokesmen were often bishops (there were exceptions, like Jerome and Origen) and the bishops generally competent theologians (like Augustine and Chrysostom). Only later times would separate the **hierarchical** magisterium from the **theological** magisterium, with unfortunate results.

Exercise of this teaching office under Constantine was sometimes affected by imperial patronage or partisan rivalry. As Emperor he wished to be patron of the Church, though still pagan in his roots, and he had the bishops assemble in the first ecumenical Council (so called because it represented all the inhabited world) of the patristic era at Nicea (in the shadow of Constantinople) in AD 325. A creed was produced, a key term (*homoousios*) decided on to defend the equality of the Word with the Father, and false hope created that these magisterial statements would once and for all settle issues to do with Christ and the correlative doctrine of the Trinity.

It was a vain hope: spokesmen from all points of the theological spectrum quoted the creeds and formulas in senses to suit themselves and claimed the authority of the New Testament. This continued to be the case despite the meeting of bishops in **ecumenical Council** at Constantinople in AD 381 (giving us our present Nicene–Constantinopolitan Creed — see Appendix for text), at Ephesus in AD 431, and at Chalcedon in AD 451 — all in the far East, away from the patriarch of Rome, the Pope. Dispute and confusion continued because theological difficulties had not been settled before definition was made at another level (as would occur also in modern times).

Whatever the atmosphere of these Councils, theological debate (to which the West, with its interest more in discipline, made little contribution) was conducted with great acrimony, largely arising out of rivalries between cities/patriarchates/schools of exegesis/philosophical systems. So the task of dealing with the unique challenge that Christ presented, true God and true man, was made more difficult by local imbalance in favour of either divinity or humanity, as well as racial/historical concerns for monotheism or distinction in Christ. The **Alexandrian** school, Jewish in its origins, naturally emphasised the former and was impatient of the kind of progressive theologising that explored distinction in

Christ, as was possible at **Antioch**. The latter centre rested on pragmatic Aristotelian **philosophy** for its theologising, Alexandria on the more speculative Platonic philosophy. Further, though all contributors to the debate spoke Greek, key terms took on different meanings depending on the different philosophies of the speakers. Theology would always have a **language** problem.

So it is not surprising that when this series of Councils dealing with unity and distinction in Christ reached a climax at Chalcedon in AD 451, theological debate did not cease, despite the tone of finality of the formula arrived at. Though the hierarchical magisterium has not since then attempted any improved **definition**, Christological discussion continued and later councils offered instead **descriptive** statements, like those of Vatican II.

The Chalcedonian formula

Following therefore the holy Fathers we unanimously teach that the Son, our Lord Jesus Christ, is one and the same, the same perfect in divinity, the same perfect in humanity, true God and true man, consisting of a rational soul and a body, consubstantial with the Father in divinity and consubstantial with us in humanity, 'in all things like as we are, without sin' (*Heb* 4.15), born of the Father before all time as to his divinity, born in recent times for us and for our salvation from the Virgin Mary, Mother of God, as to his humanity.

We confess one and the same Christ, the Son, the Lord, the only-begotten, in two natures unconfused, unchangeable, undivided and inseparable. The difference of natures will never be abolished by their being united, but rather the properties of each remain unimpaired, both coming together in one person and substance, not parted or divided among two persons, but in one and the same only-begotten Son, the divine Word, the Lord Jesus Christ, as previously the prophets and Jesus Christ himself taught us and the Creed of the Fathers handed down to us . . . The above having been considered with all and every care and diligence, this Holy Ecumenical Council has defined that no one may advance any other belief or inscribe, compose, hold or teach it in any other way.

This statement and other early creeds and formulas show theology and hierarchical magisterium meeting in the process of transmitting those foundational experiences of the community. It has not always been a happy meeting, especially since the patristic age, which at least enjoyed the advantage of having hierarchical teachers who were competent theologians, like Athanasius and Pope Leo (who were nonetheless not free of human bias). Both theologians and hierarchical teachers serve the same end in the community's search for the revealed and saving experience, even if in recent times the tendency has been to divorce theology from magisterium. **Theology**, as St Anselm pointed out in the eleventh century, asks the questions that lead to a more exact and sophisticated understanding of the faith; it is the task of **hierarchical** teachers (who hopefully, like their patristic counterparts, are more than mere administrators) to proclaim and explain the faith of the community to its members. Each makes a contribution, so that it may be said that the theological investigation of one generation can become hierarchical teaching in another generation.

How helpful are statements like Chalcedon's? How much are the community brought through them to share dependently in the foundational **experience**? Does their expression prove **revelatory** (and **saving**) for the community at all levels (and not just 'churchmen')? Reciting our creeds is an exercise of tradition, **doctrinal** tradition, passing on our beliefs from one generation to the next. We must ensure that this one form of tradition is seen to correspond also with **biblical**, **liturgical** and **catechetical** forms of tradition if the teaching (magisterium) is to be authentic.

The late Karl Rahner, in an article entitled 'Chalcedon — end or beginning?', suggests such statements are both:

> Work by the theologians and teachers of the Church bearing on a reality and a truth revealed by God always ends in an exact formulation. This is natural and necessary. For only in this way is it possible to draw a line of demarcation, excluding heresy and misunderstanding of the divine truth, which can be observed in everyday religious practice. But if the formula is thus an end, the result and victory which bring about simplicity, clarity, the possibility of teaching and doctrinal certainty, then in this victory everything depends on the end also being seen as a beginning.

Tradition must constantly serve the reality, the mystery, the experience — not imprison it. Hence the justification for the work of theologians.

Some relevant reading

Adam, K., *The Christ of Faith*, Burns and Oates, London, 1957.

Dulles, A., *A Church to Believe in*, Crossroad, New York, 1982 (Chapters 7, 8).

Fuller, R. H., *The Foundations of New Testament Christology*, Collins, London, 1965.

Grillmeier, A., *Christ in Christian Tradition* I, (2nd edn), Mowbray, London, 1975.

Malone, P., 'Controversy in the Church'. *Compass Theology Review* 15 (1981, Autumn) 1–9.

O'Collins, G., *Fundamental Theology*, Paulist, New York, 1981 (Chapters 6, 7, 8).

Exercises in theology

(1) Each Sunday we recite the Creed of Nicea and Constantinople. Does that recital really function as an example of doctrinal tradition, handing on quite precise statements about Christ's humanity and divinity in such a way as to bring us a share in basic Christian experiences? Are there better situations for employing credal statements of our beliefs (see Appendix for text of Creeds)?

(2) Language is a continuing problem for theologians struggling to express belief precisely. The bishops of Nicea thought *homoousios* might settle debate about Jesus, but people interpreted it differently. Our time has certain terms that are used ambiguously, like 'humanism', 'liberation'. Can you think of others? How important is precision in theological statement? What does a reading of the New Testament suggest?

(3) In the patristic age theologians were generally bishops, and bishops theologians; both exercised magisterium. In the Middle Ages theologians attended Councils with bishops and decided questions of othodoxy (see Dulles on this). What effects have you noticed in your reading of the more recent tendency to divorce the two forms of teaching in the community?

6

The experience at risk in systematic transmission: Scholastic theology

Theology to be valid has to keep in close touch with the experience of God in those foundational words and events that proved revelatory and saving for the community and for the individual. Paul placed great stress on the early Church's preoccupation with the Paschal Mystery, and he himself had his own experience to remember. The Fathers generally pondered and explained the way these experiences had been transmitted in biblical and liturgical forms, though necessarily putting some reliance on current philosophies to organise and communicate their ideas. The Councils of the patristic golden age also invoked the language of current philosophy to devise 'adequate' formulas to transmit the **foundational experiences**, perhaps not always reaching the 'simple faithful' thereby.

We had occasion to notice, in fact, that already in conciliar theology something of that desirable closeness of touch with the foundational experience was fading. There had been a **shift in emphasis**, for instance, from the Paschal Mystery in

Jesus' life to his Incarnation, the moment of the union of the two natures that was so much under the microscope from Nicea to Chalcedon; for these Councils what Jesus *is* became of greater importance than what he *does*, unlike the focus of interest in the Scriptures, the God who acts. Thus there comes about a **parting of the ways** of dogmatic tradition about Jesus from biblical and liturgical forms of tradition of the experience. Movement from narrative (biblical) **language** in the dogmatic formulas to more sophisticated (and ambiguous) expression helped reduce their intelligibility and impair the process of tradition.

Commentary on biblical texts, so dear to the Fathers, and isolated dogmatic pronouncements from the hierarchical magisterium, however, would not satisfy theological minds wanting a conspectus (or *summa*) of the whole Christian mystery. Hence the medieval period that followed the close of the patristic era saw the rise of the great **systematic theologians** of the West, beginning with Anselm in the eleventh century and culminating in Thomas Aquinas and the dominance of **Scholasticism**. The contribution of 'Scholastic' theology — produced in schools (such as the great medieval universities of Paris, Oxford and Bologna) by teachers for their students — was to bring system to theology. The question is whether the system adopted did justice to all dimensions of the reality.

A great contemporary exponent of Scholasticism, M. D. Chenu OP, reminds us that the West had already by the time of Aquinas lost some of the perspective retained by Eastern theologians: 'It is a fact that every time this oriental theology filters westward it is at once received with reserve, sometimes with hostility. Its cosmic and Christological optimism is rather shocking to the mind of the West, dominated as it is by the Augustinian view of the universe and of sinful humanity'. The system that St Thomas applies is based on another philosophical notion, the Neoplatonic pattern of the emanation of all things from God and their return to him — *exitus* and *reditus* in St Thomas's Latin. So his *Summa Theologiae* deals in Part I with God and creation (the *exitus*), and in Part II with the human being's way of returning to God (the theology of human behaviour — moral theology), Part III presenting Christ and the sacraments as a different dimension for the Christian life already covered in Part II. It is a magnificent synthesis of faith and reason, characterised also by its integrity in relating all created realities to God (who nevertheless can be known rather for what he is not than for what he is, as the *Summa* reminds us at its opening).

The pattern, we would observe, is not directly related to the OT cultic credos or the Paschal Mystery, though Chenu asserts the *Summa* was in fact founded simply upon a commentary on the Gospels which was included in the ordinary course of study for Dominican teachers in the universities of Paris and Naples. As always with theology, the question one has to ask of St Thomas's *Summa* (as of any theologian's system) is: how well is the community's experience being transmitted, how far does it square with other forms of tradition — biblical, liturgical, etc? The *exitus–reditus* pattern allows Christ to appear only in Part III, introduced in the prologue in these words:

Our Saviour, the Lord Jesus Christ, in order to save his people from their sins, as the angel testifies (*Mt* 1.21), showed to us in his very person the way of truth, whereby by rising again we may reach the beatitude of immortal life. Hence it is necessary for the completion of the work of theology that we should now consider, after our study of the ultimate end of human life and of the virtues and vices, the Saviour of all people and the benefits bestowed by him on the human race.

In this connection there is need to consider firstly the Saviour himself; secondly his sacraments, which are the means by which we attain salvation; thirdly the goal of immortal life, which we reach by rising through him.

On the first of these points is a twofold consideration: the first deals with the very mystery of the Incarnation, by which God became man for our salvation; the second deals with the things that were done and suffered by our Saviour himself, that is, God incarnate.

One suspects Paul would not be happy with **the way the emphasis falls**, whatever the comprehensiveness of the pattern and its logic. Further, some of the discredit that Scholasticism has (unfairly?) earned can be explained by passages from the *Summa*, such as the following on angels in Part I (from the fourteen questions devoted to angels there, more than the space given to the Paschal Mystery — in III!); Thomas is discussing the rather rarefied question ('of first importance', would Paul agree?) of whether angels obtained grace and glory to the degree of their natural gifts:

My reply is that we must admit it is logical that the angels were given gifts of grace and the perfection of beatitude in proportion to their natural gifts. The reason for this is twofold. First of all, on the part of God himself, who in the order established by his wisdom sets up various degrees of angelic nature. Inasmuch as angelic nature was made by God to attain grace and beatitude, so also the grades of that nature seem to be ordained to the various degrees of grace and glory. So, for example, when a builder chisels stones to construct a house, from the very fact that he prepares some more artistically and more symmetrically it is clear that he intends them for the finer parts of the house. It therefore seems that God destined to greater gifts of grace and fuller beatitude the angels he made of a higher nature.

The same conclusion is evident on the part of the angel . . . From this it appears that the angels who had greater natural gifts had more of grace and glory.

(Part I, q. 62, a. 6)

Perhaps one can see how the biblical and liturgical forms of transmitting the foundational experiences fell into some decay in medieval times, and how theology could lose its roots. It is not surprising, therefore, that when Vatican II reviews the studies of seminarians, it is not content simply to repeat the age-old endorsement of 'the Angelic Doctor' but insists that **Thomistic method** needs to be set within a sound tradition of those foundational experiences that emerge more conspicuously in the Bible and the liturgy:

The theological disciplines should be communicated in the light of faith under the guidance of the Church's magisterium and in such a way that students will draw Catholic doctrine accurately from divine revelation, penetrate it in depth, derive nourishment for their own spiritual life and be in a position to proclaim, expound and defend it in their priestly ministry.

Students should be instructed with particular diligence in the study of Sacred Scripture, which ought to be the soul of all theology, as it were. Following a suitable introduction to it, they should be carefully initiated in exegetical method, discerning the great themes of divine revelation and gaining inspiration and nourishment from daily reading and meditation on the Sacred Books.

Dogmatic theology should be arranged in such a way that those biblical themes are presented first. Students should be made aware of the contribution of the Fathers of the Church from East

34

and West to the faithful transmission and explication of each truth of revelation, as also the later history of dogma and as well its relation to the overall history of the Church. Then, for a comprehensive illustration of the mysteries of salvation to the extent possible, the students should learn, with the help of speculative reason under the guidance of St Thomas, to penetrate them more deeply and grasp their interrelation. These they ought be taught to recognise ever present and active in liturgical actions and the whole life of the Church. Let them learn to look for solutions to human problems in the light of revelation, to apply eternal truths to the changing condition of human affairs, and to communicate them in a manner suited to their contemporaries.

(Decree on Priestly Formation 16)

Before Vatican II, theology in Catholic seminaries had generally been taught on a Scholastic model under the influence of Aquinas. Today, however, a **range of theological methods** are available, some pioneered by Catholic theologians; they go by names such as anthropological, empirical, existential, transcendental, and themselves invoke the help of various philosophical systems (just as Aquinas benefited from Aristotelian philosophy). The recently deceased Jesuit theologian, Karl Rahner, for instance, dominated the contemporary scene in the way Aquinas did his. Rahner's theology begins with the experience of the human being (and hence is anthropological rather than God-centred) but the human being as radically open to God (and hence is transcendental); that is a different starting point from those who would see revelation rather as a predetermined set of propositions unaffected by the human situation. Bernard Lonergan, a Canadian Jesuit and as much a philosopher as a theologian, also begins with the data of experience; if theology is faith seeking understanding, Lonergan the philosopher-theologian looks hard at our ways of understanding. The **changes in 'doing theology'** that theologians like Rahner and Lonergan have brought to Catholic theology have been styled a Copernican revolution. (We will look at other changes in emphasis in theology in later chapters.)

Some relevant reading

Chenu, M. D., *Is Theology a Science?*, Burns and Oates, London, 1959.

Lonergan, B., *Method in Theology*, Herder and Herder, New York, 1972.

Mueller, J., *What are They Saying about Theological Method?*, Paulist, New York, 1984.

Powers, J., 'Confirmation: the problem of meaning', *Worship* 46 (1972) 281–91.

St Thomas Aquinas, *Summa Theologiae*, 3 vols, Blackfriars, London, 1964.

Vatican II, *Dogmatic Constitution on Divine Revelation*, Rome, 1965 (Chapter 6).

——, *Decree on Priestly Formation*, Rome, 1965 (Chapter 5).

Exercises in theology

(1) From your theological reading or experience, would you say that theology today addresses the key questions affecting Christians? Is relevance an adequate criterion for a system of theology? Did the New Testament grapple with the issues of its day?

(2) Catechetical tradition of basic Christian experiences, as much as theological tradition, has need of completeness and integrity. Comment on the adequacy of your own catechetical formation and/or teaching: are there areas of neglect or over-emphasis? Refer to the thinking of Vatican II quoted above.

(3) The medieval period that produced the great systems of theology also built the cathedrals of Europe. Admirable as they are, they tend to lose the 'simple faithful' in their very grandeur. Has the modern renewal of the liturgy adjusted that imbalance for you, thanks to your efforts to be part of it? Do you really take pains to make the liturgy live for you and your students?

7

Reforming the community by pruning its tradition: the Reformers

The lapse of time brings to the Christian community the risk of losing touch with its foundational experiences; these it continually looks for in a variety of processes and forms of tradition. Even at the hands of the evangelists and the other New Testament authors the basic experiences underwent transformation in the course of transmission, and we are the richer for the pluralist theologies of the New Testament: no other body of ancient literature provides the range of viewpoints on a historical figure that our four Gospels and other New Testament writings do. As the Christian community developed **diversity** in East and West without interrupting a rich cross-fertilisation of traditions, the Church was again enriched by diverse schools of exegesis, diverse theological emphases and doctrinal formulations, diverse liturgical expressions, and diversity in other traditional processes and forms. Augustine of Hippo and Chrysostom of Antioch both, Roman missal and Byzantine liturgy, Western discipline and Eastern speculation — all made their legitimate contribution to the variegated Tradition of Christianity, even if a case could be made for varying **degrees of adequacy and authenticity** amongst the various contributions.

As time elapsed further, as the Western half of Christendom lost living interchange with the East, following the schism between Rome and Constantinople in the eleventh century, as a range of factors led to ebb and flow of vitality in the various channels of tradition flowing from foundational experiences, the dangers of **theological imbalance and decadence** were inevitably realised in practice. Even if the thirteenth was 'the greatest of the centuries', and theology shared in the greatness to the extent of benefiting from the systems of Aquinas and Duns Scotus, it still awaited the rebirth of classical learning that could bring new life to study of **the Scriptures**, knowledge of original languages and other skills having fallen away. **Liturgy**, sacramental devotion and expressions of **piety** became marked by exaggeration and imbalance, such as a loss of a Paschal perspective, undue Eucharistic realism and improper emphasis in penitential practice, sentimentality and emotionalism in forms of piety, a growing gap between vernacular languages and Latin Scriptures. Church **structures** also lost some of the spirit of the Gospels. All this reflected an inadequate theology arising from impaired transmission of Christianity's foundational experiences.

Small wonder that the need for restoration of a true emphasis and more authentic contact with the origins — reform — was widely voiced. A coincidence of factors thrust an Augustinian theologian and scriptural translator, Martin Luther, into a position of influence in the movement for reform in the sixteenth century, in the wake of a new learning that made possible some means of return to the sources. His scriptural interests and rejection of certain Roman doctrinal and sacramental positions led this **Reformation** movement to centre on debate over relative priority of scriptural, dogmatic and liturgical forms of tradition, culminating not simply in a general return to pristine authenticity in all traditions but exclusive preference for one: *Scriptura sola* became (and remains) the talisman of Reformation theology.

We do not condemn the doctrines of men just because they are the doctrines of men, for we would gladly put up with them. But we condemn them because they are contrary to the gospel and the Scriptures. While the Scriptures liberate consciences and forbid that they be taken captive by the doctrines of men, these doctrines of men captivate the conscience anyhow. This conflict between the Scriptures and the doctrines of men we cannot reconcile. Therefore because these two forms of doctrine contradict one another we allow even young children to judge here whether we are to give up the Scriptures, in which the one Word of God is taught from the beginning of the world, or whether we are to give up the doctrines of men, which were newly devised yesterday and which change daily?

We hope that everyone will agree with the decision that the doctrines of men must be forsaken and the Scriptures retained. For they will neither desire nor be able to keep both, since the two cannot be reconciled and are by nature necessarily opposed to one another, like fire and water, like heaven and earth. As Isaiah 55[:9] puts it, 'As the heavens are higher than the earth, so are my ways higher than your ways.' Now he who walks on the earth cannot at the same time walk in heaven, and he who walks in heaven cannot walk on the earth.

Therefore we request the papists that they first reconcile their doctrine with the Scriptures. If they accomplish that, we will observe their doctrines. But that they will not do until the Holy Spirit first becomes a liar. Therefore we say again: We censure the doctrines of men not because men have spoken them, but because they are lies and blasphemies against the Scriptures. And the Scriptures, although they too are written by men, are neither of men nor from men but from God. Now since Scriptures and the doctrines of men are contrary one to the other, the one must lie and the other be true. Now let us see to which of the two the papists themselves will ascribe the lie.

Let this be enough.

(Luther, *On avoiding the doctrines of men*)

In short, a movement for pruning decay from the processes of Christian tradition culminated in the pruning of some of these legitimate processes themselves — not just unwanted growth but the very branches. The Reformers elevated the Bible to a position of pre-eminence, depressing (if not eliminating) the role of liturgy and Church dogma; and Lutheran Scripture scholars such as Ernst Käsemann still write in that vein today:

Of course, it is self-evident that Christian fellowships and churches look to Scripture. But this can be done in very different ways. The distinguishing mark of the Reformation and its disciples is the exclusive particle, the word 'alone' . . .

39

It will not be unfair if we sum up the ideal of piety among Protestant congregations in the formula: every man sitting down with his Bible in front of him! Undoubtedly this conception does point towards the Church as the hearing and obeying community.

(Käsemann, *Thoughts on the present controversy about scriptural interpretation*, 1969)

It was a case of one imbalance provoking another — and yet another as **Counter-Reform** swung in the opposite direction: Reformists' promotion of Scripture to the detriment of the (other) sacraments and liturgy in general had the knee-jerk effect in Rome of depressing the importance of Bible study and creating a false distinction between 'Scripture and tradition' (spoken of in Chapter 2). So a proper understanding of the respective processes of the community's tradition of foundational experiences remained deficient, and was further complicated by the additional **division** of the community's life — the lived tradition. The Christian West, already sundered from the Orthodox East, was now itself divided into hostile communities. Only with Vatican II would the Catholic community endeavour to right the former deficiency by rethinking the notion of Tradition and traditions; repair of divisions is a lengthier process.

Some relevant reading

Brown, R. E., 'Moving the Churches to Reform', *The Critical Meaning of the Bible*, Chapman, London, 1982, pp. 107–23.

Congar, Y., *Diversity and Communion*, Twenty Third Publications, Mystic, 1985.

Hendrix, S., 'Luther against the background of the history of biblical interpretation', *Interpretation* 37 (1983) 229–39.

Käsemann, E., *New Testament Questions of Today*, (2nd edn), SCM Press, London, 1969.

Luther, M., *Works*, Volume 35, ed. E. Bachmann, Fortress, Philadelphia, 1960.

Exercises in theology

(1) We tend to identify Christianity with our local form of Catholicism, ignoring the diversity of Christian tradition. Perhaps ecumenism and a growing multiculturalism in many societies are alerting us to some aspects of this diversity. List the diverse Christian traditions (not simply Western) that exist and are available for reference in your locality.

(2) How much room for diversity and pluralism is there in the Christian community? How much uniformity? At what point does diversity mean losing touch with the experiences that are foundational for the community? Is that the only criterion for determining a legitimate degree of diversity in the life of the community? Point to the evidence in history.

(3) From Reformation times and even before, for reasons explained above, Catholics have lost some contact with the biblical tradition of Christianity, and stand in need of 'reformation' to that extent. Do you see any evidence of this in your own case or among Catholics generally in matters of homilies at Mass, scriptural character of religious education programs, structure of College courses, forms of piety, etc.?

8

Evaluating

the community's

tradition:

Biblical criticism

In the sixteenth century the Christian tradition in the West underwent a painful period of theological re-evaluation that was due to the Reformers and that we know as the Reformation. In a nutshell, they put to the community the question: how adequate a communication of the foundational experiences do we receive from forms of tradition that are largely doctrinal (even if beautifully systematised), liturgical, catechetical, and not principally biblical? As often happens with human responses under stress, the positions taken were extreme: on the one hand, the cry *Scriptura sola* of the Reformers, as though no other form of transmission did justice to the experience; on the other, an assertion that 'not only Scripture but also Tradition' contained the truth, as though these were mutually exclusive.

The polemical atmosphere of the time also produced an **imbalance** in studying biblical tradition. For Luther and other Reformers, opposed to current Church practice on indulgences and its relation to a theology of grace, Pauline teaching on justification assumed an exaggerated importance that distorted the presentation of Paul's basic missionary concerns and even depressed the role of the Gospels in Christian tradition. 'In the Scholastics I lost Christ', lamented Luther, 'but found him again in Paul' — not in the Gospels, significantly. In England the poet John Donne mirrored this esteem: 'Wheresoever I open St Paul's epistles, I meet not words but thunder, and universal thunder, thunder that passes through all the world.'

It was left for the eighteenth and nineteenth centuries to **rediscover the Gospels**, at least the Synoptics, along with a realisation that amidst the Reformation debates the portrait of Jesus had been allowed to slip from the focus of attention. Hence a rash of 'Lives of Jesus' based on a mining of Gospel texts for insights into Jesus' personality, not always as much interested in dogmatic as in psychological features, as was true of Renan's famous *Life of Jesus* in 1863. More critical yet basically sympathetic approaches were adopted by biblical scholars, such as Albert Schweitzer, whose *The Quest of the Historical Jesus* in 1906 gave respectability to the search for Jesus' vital statistics in the Gospels.

It took more than religious developments to question the validity of this whole approach to Scripture and put a stop to the 'Lives of Jesus' that treated the Gospels as history pure and simple, psychology or even romance. In the first third of the twentieth century there occurred a **total re-evaluation of biblical tradition** amongst those for whom the Bible was everything (the Catholics being less affected by scholarly developments because they were out of touch with them, and Anglican scholars being less subject to German extravagances). What contributed to this re-evaluation of Scripture and thus to a repudiation of the quest for the historical Jesus were developments in the overall study of history and the military and economic collapse of Germany with the First World War. Historiography took on a positivistic slant, disallowing anything subjective in historical composition and therefore disqualifying documents like Gospel portraits of Jesus that could not be verified by these historians' (one-sided) criteria.

Influenced by this approach and affected by the collapse of his world in post-war Germany, Rudolph Bultmann, professor in Marburg, initiated a review of Gospel material that went beyond the long-standing acceptance of diversity of sources and authors (the object of literary criticism) recognised for centuries in the case of Old Testament material (see Chapter 2). Bultmann proceeded to apply as well the principles of *form criticism* that showed the evangelists as manipulators of pre-formed material, and thus discounted any simple approach to finding a biography of Jesus in the Gospels:

Critical investigation shows that the whole tradition about Jesus which appears in the three synoptic gospels is composed of a series of layers which can on the whole be clearly distinguished, although the separation at some points is difficult and doubtful. *(The Gospel of John cannot be taken into account at all* as a source for the teaching of Jesus, and it is not referred to in this book). The separating of these layers in the synoptic gospels depends on the knowledge that these gospels were composed in Greek within the Hellenistic Christian community, while Jesus and the oldest Christian group lived in Palestine and spoke Aramaic. Hence everything in the synoptics which for reasons of language or content can have originated only in Hellenistic Christianity must be excluded as a source for the teaching of Jesus. The critical analysis shows, however, that the essential content of these three gospels was taken over from the Aramaic tradition of the oldest Palestinian community. Within this Palestinian material again different layers can be distinguished, in which whatever betrays the specific interests of the church or reveals characteristics of later development must be rejected as secondary. By means of this critical analysis an oldest layer is determined, though it can be marked off with only relative exactness. *Naturally we have no absolute assurance that the exact words of this oldest layer were really spoken by Jesus.* There is a possibility that the contents of this oldest layer are also the result of a complicated historical process which we can no longer trace.

Of course the doubt as to whether Jesus really existed is unfounded and not worth refutation. No sane person can doubt that Jesus stands as founder behind the historical movement whose first distinct stage is represented by the oldest Palestinian community. *But how far that community preserved an objectively true picture of him and his message is another question.* For those whose interest is in the personality of Jesus, this situation is depressing or destructive; for our purpose it has no particular significance. It is precisely this complex of ideas in the oldest layer of the synoptic tradition which is the object of our consideration. It meets us as a fragment of tradition coming to us from the past, and in the examination of it we seek the encounter with history. By the tradition Jesus is named as bearer of the message; according to overwhelming probability he really was. Should it prove otherwise, that does not change in any way what is said in the record. I see then no objection to naming Jesus throughout as the speaker. Whoever prefers to put the name of 'Jesus' always in quotation marks and let it stand as an abbreviation for the historical phenomenon with which we are concerned, is free to do so.

(R. Bultmann, Jesus and the Word, 1934, my emphases)

The impact of this 'form-history method' was immense: if the gospels could not be taken at face value, what could? Evangelical Protestants, with their strongly biblical background and suspicion of other forms of tradition, were particularly devastated. Bultmann and his followers (Bultmannians) were scholars of high religious motivation, and their work of **'demythologising'** (or recognising the presence of figurative overlay — 'myth' — in biblical material) fundamentally sound. But in the circumstances of the time, and with the influence also of the contemporary existentialist philosophy of Heidegger that raised other vast questions about reality, a wave of agnosticism swept Europe: belief became too risky an option. In the wake of a second world war a 'God is dead' theology developed that depersonalised the whole notion of God. People whose faith was nourished on the Bible alone, deprived of sound liturgical and doctrinal traditions, found themselves cut off from the Christian experience.

Some light in the darkness was shed by the great post-Bultmannians — scholars like Käsemann, Bornkamm and Conzelmann, who had had second thoughts with the development of historiography and admitted the role of the subjective in a historian. In place of a positivistic approach to New Testament history, it was possible to take a theological approach and to recognise the independent theological role of each evangelist presenting Jesus differently (a scandal to positivistic historians) according to the circumstances and purposes of each; redaction criticism now centred on this editorial work of the theologian-evangelists. A new quest of the historical Jesus thus became possible.

That the impact of these successive waves was not universal in Christendom was due partly to the less extreme, more consistent, if less original work of great English non-Catholic scholars such as C. H. Dodd, T. W. Manson, Vincent Taylor and W. D. Davies. The Catholic community, out of the mainstream of biblical scholarship for historical reasons and reliant also on other forms of tradition, were largely unaware of the storm, and continued to read their lives of Jesus and express their faith in devotional (if unbiblical) forms. It was only with the Pontifical Biblical Commission's 1964 Instruction on the Historical Value of the Gospels and Vatican II's Constitution on Divine Revelation (1965) that they were introduced to some of the fruits of the scholarship that had subjected biblical tradition to such searching re-evaluation.

Close scrutiny of tradition like this by theologians is necessary, though painful, if the community's foundational experiences are to be adequately transmitted and responded to in a
sound faith. The Catholic community in the West also submitted its liturgical tradition to review and adjustment in this
century under the guidance of people like Pope Pius X and
Joseph Jungmann. Its doctrinal tradition would likewise
undergo review in the mid-twentieth century during a new
general council. Needless to say, the painfulness of these
review processes is less extreme the closer the dialogue in the
community between investigative theologians and other
Church teachers.

Some relevant reading

Bultmann, R., *The History of the Synoptic Tradition*, (2nd edn),
    Blackwell, Oxford, 1968.
Collins, R. F., *Introduction to the New Testament*, Doubleday,
    New York, 1983.
McArthur, H. (ed.), *In Search of the Historical Jesus*, SPCK,
    London, 1970.
Pontifical Biblical Commission, *Instruction on the Historical
    Value of the Gospels*, Rome, 1964.
Robinson, J. A. T., *Honest to God*, SCM Press, London, 1963.
Vatican II, *Dogmatic Constitution on Divine Revelation*, Rome,
    1965.

Exercises in theology

(1) Examine a life of Jesus you know, from the library or on
film. How does it establish its portrait of Jesus from Gospel
material? Does it stress physical and psychological features of
Jesus on which the evangelists do not offer information? Does
it restrict itself to historical data that can be authenticated
from other sources? Or does it take the viewpoint of particular evangelists and thus avoid a fixed stereotype?

(2) Bultmann has been shown above discrediting the Gospel
of John and relying solely on the Synoptics. From your

reading of the various Gospels, why would you say he and others could have easily arrived at this position? What effect on a theology of Jesus occurs (a) if John is excluded, (b) if he is included by a theologian of the New Testament?

(3) Distinguish the sense of 'myth' as employed by biblical scholars from its use in English generally. Why do you think its use in regard to the Bible worries some people, so that even scholars like Raymond Brown avoid using it? Does the Biblical Commission's Instruction support the notion of demythologising practised by readers of the Gospels (see Appendix for text of Instruction)?

9

Relating

the experience

to the times:

Vatican II

In two millennia the Christian community had not only been distanced greatly from its foundational experiences but had expanded into a vast number of adherents and spread across the whole globe in a great diversity of races, cultures, regions and languages. The Church that the early leaders reviewed at the Council of Jerusalem in AD 49 bore almost no resemblance to that reviewed by the two thousand prelates at the Second Vatican Council in Rome in 1962–65. What characterised the intervening period was change, development.

Characteristic of the modern world and society as a whole is the rate of change and development, certainly by comparison with the world of the early Church Councils. Whereas the world at the time of Chalcedon in AD 451 did not differ greatly in extent and cultures from that of Jerusalem in AD 49, the holding of modern Church Councils by no means kept pace with the **rate of change** in world and society, so that a totally different community presented itself for review on each occasion. Three hundred years had elapsed between **Trent** in the mid-sixteenth century and **Vatican I** in the mid-nineteenth, and in that time the whole face of Europe had altered and the New World had been occupied, not to mention the religious diversification that had occurred in the wake of the Reformation. And in the century between Vatican I and Vatican II, Europe and the whole world had been involved in many conflicts and two world wars, the effects of the Industrial Revolution had been felt world-wide, and the Third World had been colonised and decolonised to become the locus of more prosperous Church growth than the original centres.

Clearly, some new system of review of this vastly expanded community was required if the diversity of Church life was to bear also some signs of uniformity. Sociologists such as Alvin Toffler in his book *Future Shock* reminded us of the accelerating pace of change and development: almost as much had happened since we were born (they told us) as had happened to the world since the beginning of time. The ease and speed of communication had increased remarkably: whereas prior to the sixteenth century Europe produced one thousand new books a year, today the figure is two hundred times as great — and electronic means of communication have turned the world into a global village.

So when the bishops gathered in Rome in 1962 for the opening of Vatican II, the challenge of the review of community life and tradition as well as the possibilities of achieving it were immense. Unlike Vatican I, conditions favoured an uninterrupted process of review. Pope John XXIII in convoking the Council saw its task as relating the Church to this rapidly changing world:

> It is a question in fact of bringing the modern world into contact with the vivifying and perennial energies of the Gospel, a world which exalts itself with its conquests in the technical and scientific fields, but which brings also the consequences of a temporal order which some have wished to reorganise excluding God.

The two thousand bishops for the first time came from all parts of the world, and for the first time revealed the Third World as the growth area of the Church; no longer could the Christian community be seen as Mediterranean or European but was truly catholic (if not ecumenical in including the Orthodox). Diversity — of languages, cultures, outlooks — marked this assembly as it marks the Church, and guaranteed a **diversity of theological viewpoints** in Council discussions — something 'monolithic' Rome was not accustomed to. How would the Council speak with one voice on the various issues?

The timeliness of this Council was seen in the **decisive and revolutionary positions** taken on basic issues (even if these were late in coming when one considers the amount of biblical and theological work done previously by other traditions and by individual Catholic theologians like Lagrange, De Lubac, Congar and Teilhard de Chardin, who had suffered for their initiative in the years before the Council). The Church was no longer seen inadequately as a human society only, but more basically as the People of God, not dominated by an ordained hierarchy but with an active laity exercising baptismal responsibilities. Within this Church the Blessed Virgin Mary was considered as Mother of the Church and first disciple. Post-Reformation hangups about two sources of revelation (Scripture and Tradition) gave way to a serene presentation of a God sharing himself in his Word, in history, in nature, in daily life, and pre-eminently in the person of Jesus. The modern world and its developments became the subject of a whole constitution, with a tone of optimism.

Though one thousand five hundred years had elapsed since Chalcedon, the Fathers of Vatican II attempted no formal **definition** on the subject of Jesus or any other aspect of the Christian event. Recent history and the experience of rapid change suggested the wisdom of **description** rather than definition, of analysis of problems rather than pat solutions, of a diversity of approaches rather than a single approach applied uniformly to all situations. The figure of Jesus therefore appears in a much more biblical description than Chalcedon's and consequently in a pluralist picture arising from the plurality of New Testament authors:

> The Truth is that only in the mystery of the incarnate Word does the mystery of man take on light. For Adam, the first man, was a figure of Him who was to come, namely, Christ the Lord. Christ, the final Adam, by the revelation of the mystery of the Father and His love, fully reveals man to man himself and makes his supreme calling clear. It is not surprising, then, that in Him all the aforementioned truths find their root and attain their crown.
>
> He who is 'the image of the invisible God' (*Col* 1.15), is Himself the perfect man. To the sons of Adam He restores the divine likeness which had been disfigured from the first sin onward. Since human nature as He assumed it was not annulled, by that very fact it has been raised up to a divine dignity in our respect too. For by His incarnation the Son of God has united Himself in some fashion with every man. He worked with human hands, He thought with a human mind, acted by human choice, and loved

50

with a human heart. Born of the Virgin Mary, He has truly been made one of us, like us in all things except sin.

As an innocent lamb He merited life for us by the free shedding of His own blood. In Him God reconciled us to Himself and among ourselves. From bondage to the devil and sin, he delivered us, so that each one of us can say with the Apostle: The Son of God 'loved me and gave himself up for me' (*Gal* 2.20). By suffering for us He not only provided us with an example for our imitation. He blazed a trail, and if we follow it, life and death are made holy and take on a new meaning.

(*The Church in the Modern World*, 22)

Not that total unanimity marked these two thousand prelates of so varied backgrounds and attitudes in their sixteen constitutions, decrees, declarations. Even after the long debates that seemed to have settled questions like the nature of the Church and of revelation, Council documents can still betray the hand of writers thinking in terms of institutional Church only, or Scripture versus tradition, or other outmoded theologies; **compromise** still marks the frontier-breaking documents on ecumenism and non-Christian religions. Not all statements are as thorough as might have been expected, such as the Declaration on Christian Education.

But at least the community had had an opportunity to review itself and the world in the light of its original experiences (as the very biblical character of its statements reveals) and to examine the authenticity of its tradition of those experiences in the many cultures where they are now transmitted. It was also agreed that, even if general Councils are rare, the *process of review* should keep pace with societal change through a system of Synod of Bishops meeting every three years. Change and development are less painful if gradual rather than delayed and abrupt — something the post-conciliar Church came to recognise as people struggled to adapt themselves to the updated teaching or, in the phrase of Pope John, *aggiornamento* (see chart).

From Trent through Vatican I to Vatican II

A world of little social change	A world of rapid social change
A world based on Europe	A world based on the Third World

The Church defines herself as perfect society, institution	The Church defines herself as mystery, people, herald, servant
The Catholic Church v. other Churches	All Churches moving together to unity
'Outside the Church no salvation' interpreted exclusively	'Outside the Church no salvation' interpreted inclusively
Church membership clearly defined	Degrees of membership
Hierarchy as monarchical government	Hierarchy as servants
The priesthood of the ordained, emphasis on Orders	The priesthood of the baptised, emphasis on ministry
Laity passive, inarticulate	Laity involved, vocal
One Church centred in Rome, Roman style universal	Local Churches individual, enculturation
Universal monolithic structure	Diversity, pluralism, experimentation
Church based on Europe	Church based on Third World
Latin liturgy: accent on uniformity, passivity	Vernacular liturgy: accent on intelligibility, involvement
Catholic life devotional	Catholic life scriptural, sacramental
Fixed, unchanging beliefs	Development, change, growth
Church embattled, siege mentality	Openness, serenity
Church apart from world	Church associated with world
Certainty, definiteness in teaching	Living with fluidity, uncertainty
'Party line' theology	Theological pluralism
Reserve about Bible study	Encouragement of Bible study
School-based religious education	Family/parish/school-based religious education
Catechism-style religious education, in classroom	Life-situation religious education, outside classroom

Some relevant reading

Rahner, K., 'Towards a fundamental theological interpretation of Vatican II', *Theological Studies* 40 (1979) 716–27.

Ratzinger, J., *Theological Highlights of Vatican II*, Paulist, Glenrock NJ, 1966.

Schillebeeckx, E., *Vatican II — The Real Achievement*, Sheed and Ward, London, 1967.

Synod of Bishops, *Final Report*, Rome, 1985.

The Documents of Vatican II, Rome, 1965.

Vorgrimmler, H. (ed.), *Commentary on the Documents of Vatican II*, 5 volumes, Herder, New York, 1967–69.

Exercises in theology

(1) With the help of sociologists like Toffler, document the relative rapidity of change and development in our lifetime. Then tease out the implications of this for theological thinking and church life.

(2) *The Documents of Vatican II* represent a great statement of the Catholic community doctrinal tradition; members of the community would be the poorer for ignoring it. How well do you know the Vatican II documents? What should you do to improve your knowledge of them? See what was said on this subject by the 1985 Synod of Bishops devoted to study of the effect of the Council twenty years later.

(3) The text suggests above that the bishops brought to Vatican II a variety of theologies and that this diversity can be detected in some documents of the Council. Choose one council document where you see different theologies operating, perhaps in conflict, perhaps with compromise.

10

Individual response and community norms: Humanae Vitae *and beyond*

From the beginning of Christianity the response of faith to the foundational experiences has been seen to have a **moral dimension:** the beliefs of Christians appear in their lives, not simply in the way they record or celebrate these experiences. As with the people of the old relationship (or covenant/ testament), who developed a distinctive lifestyle in the wake of the Sinai experience and formulated it in lengthy moral stipulations in the Book of the Covenant (*Exodus* 20–23), so the new people's response to Jesus translated itself into a moral code; the Gospels show Jesus as a sage, like didactic wisdom figures of the Old Testament, and the letters and epistles reflect on Jesus in both dogmatic and moral chapters. Paul, whom we have seen stressing the dogmatic truth of Jesus' Paschal Mystery, who inveighs against Jewish reliance on the Mosaic law and upholds Christian freedom, nonetheless substitutes the '**Law of Christ**' and has not a few particular moral stipulations of his own.

In the succeeding ages, therefore, it is not surprising to see a continuing moral dimension to Christian tradition. The Fathers, at their best, when speaking of Christian behaviour try to keep the relationship close between **the Christian and**

Jesus without becoming arbitrary in their moralising; Irenaeus, for example, in the second century speaks first of Jesus as the manifestation of the divinity and then proceeds at once to portray the Christian as also having that exemplary role:

> The Word makes God visible to human beings in his countless mysteries lest they, totally deprived of the vision of God, lose hold of his very existence. For the glory of God is the human being fully alive, and the life of the human being is the vision of God.

> (*Against Heresies*, IV 7)

Jesus in his perfect humanity brings God clearly to us, and we have that role in our lives, too, if we live them to the full. It is a **positive morality**, drawing moral conclusions directly from the basic Christian event.

Unfortunately, that close relationship between morality and dogmatic truth was not always preserved, particularly in the West with its interest more in Church discipline than dogmatic speculation. Even the great Augustine, with his wayward youth as described at length in the *Confessions* ever before him, brings about a preoccupation with sin that stays with Christianity if only because of Augustine's lasting influence. A great Eastern commentator on the Bible like John Chrysostom could also be moralistic in his treatment of truths that the Bible itself presents as rather of dogmatic significance; for him the Fall is less significant as a crisis in human history than as an instance of the sloth or indifference he is always criticising in his congregation — so Adam is of less moment than Eve or Cain, who both exemplify that indifference. Eve (as a woman — a **sexist** slant that also will continue in Christian moral tradition) is particularly at fault:

> Why did you make your husband a partner in this grievous disaster, why prove to be the temptress of the person whose helpmate you were intended to be, and why for a tiny morsel alienate him along with yourself from the favour of God? What excess of folly led you to such heights of presumption? Wasn't it sufficient for you to pass your life without care or concern, clad in a body yet free of any bodily needs? to enjoy everything in the garden except for one tree? to have all visible things under your own authority and to exercise control over them all? Did you instead, deceived as you were by vain hopes, set your heart on reaching the very pinnacle of power?

> (Homily 16 on Genesis)

The great systematic theologians of the Middle Ages like Thomas Aquinas gave ample treatment to Christian morality; the second part, the largest, of his *Summa* is devoted to morality, and though as a Scholastic he intends to comment to his students on the Bible and the Fathers, the product is a lengthy systematisation conspicuous for symmetry and Aristotelian philosophy rather than relationship to the basic Christian experiences. He moves from a consideration of our final goal to the means of attaining it: human acts, including the passions, then the principles of human acts — habits and virtues, sin and vice, law and grace; next the theological and cardinal virtues. (Jesus, his Paschal Mystery, the sacraments come later in his work, as we have seen.) Amidst the intricacies of the beautiful system we lose the directness of Irenaeus's **relationship of Jesus and the Christian**, and can perhaps sympathise with Luther's remark, 'In the Scholastics I lost Christ'.

The Middle Ages were also a time when theological **magisterium** and hierarchical magisterium in the Church were closely aligned (see Chapter 5); bishops and (other) theologians saw eye-to-eye, and taught the people as they themselves were taught in the Schools. Pronouncements by the hierarchy on a matter such as the lending of money for interest — usury — were made in the light of Scholastic philosophy and theology, where money was seen as only a means of exchange, not of investment. Such condemnations would later be reversed as society developed a commercial mentality. Also in the Middle Ages, for the reason of that same lack of direct contact with the foundational experiences, Church practice of the sacraments took on a casuistic and legalistic character; for example, manuals for use in Confession dealt with **categories of sin** and their penalties, losing a biblical notion of reconciliation that would also one day have to be recovered. In this period, too, are made the great collections of Church law.

With the passage of time and the review of biblical and liturgical traditions of Christianity, the call came for **changes in moral theology** stemming from the clearer vision now available of those experiences basic to Christian living. Biblical criticism made possible an Old Testament theology based on a covenant in which God is beneficent Lord of a responsive people, where Gospel always precedes Law, where 'Ten Commandments' are only part of a covenant formula that begins with a recital of divine initiative and invites the response of a moral life. In the New Testament stress was given to the Paschal Mystery, the Risen Christ and Christian freedom, less to an arbitrary morality. And so the twentieth century saw the development of more biblically based moral theologies highlighting **covenant and response** rather than arbitrary law, and calling in the Christian for responsibility, formation of conscience and the use of freedom.

By the twentieth century, also, other factors had occurred that raised problems for moral theologians and Christians generally. The divorce of theology from hierarchical magisterium spoken of in Chapter 5 meant that official statements were not necessarily infused with the newer theological viewpoints. And yet a host of **old and new questions** called for restated or revised guidance if Christians were to live a life of authentic faith response, particularly in matters of bioethics and life in a just, peaceful society. The Second Vatican Council drastically revised former Church statements on religious freedom and stressed the importance of the individual's conscience in moral decision-making. The way was open for **pluralism** in moral thinking.

One the most urgent calls for guidance came in the area of **medico-moral problems** and in particular bioethics. For a century the Holy See had been publishing directives on abortion, artificial insemination, amputation, sex education, sterilisation. Pope Pius XII during his pontificate regularly addressed these issues in speaking to gatherings of the medical profession — physicians, midwives, obstetricians, anaesthetists. The issue of birth control called for particular guidance. Pius XI and Pius XII had restated the traditional teaching that every marriage act must remain open to the transmission of life. Pope John XXIII formed a study commission in 1963 composed of a range of theologians and other experts to review the question. A final report of the commission to Pope Paul VI in 1966 recommended a change in the traditional teaching to allow contraception under certain conditions; a minority report disagreed. To the comfort of many Catholic partners and the disappointment of others, Paul VI in 1968 published an encyclical reaffirming the traditional teaching:

The Church, calling people back to the observance of the natural law, as interpreted by her constant doctrine, teaches that each and every marriage act must of itself remain open to the transmission of life. That teaching, often set forth by the magisterium, is founded upon the inseparable connection, which is willed by God

57

and cannot be broken by human beings on their own initiative, between the two meanings of the conjugal act: the unitive meaning and the procreative meaning. Indeed, by its intimate structure the conjugal act, while most closely uniting husband and wife, makes them capable of generating new lives, according to laws inscribed in the very being of man and woman.

(Humanae Vitae 11, 12)

In the new post-conciliar climate, following review of the Catholic community's moral tradition in the wake of modern biblical studies, with the new emphasis on religious freedom and the development of a plurality of moral theologies, this magisterial statement was not accepted by all Catholics as definitive, and **dissent** was more public than ever before. Amongst moral theologians there were those who had difficulty with recourse to absolute moral norms; others invoked a principle of 'gradualness' to leave room for those couples not yet capable of reaching Gospel ideals. Even episcopal conferences in some countries stressed the multiplicity of factors that are involved in decision-making on this matter, such as individual conscience.

Humanae Vitae was followed in 1975 by a *Declaration on Certain Questions concerning Sexual Ethics* from the Congregation for the Doctrine of the Faith (previously the Holy Office), which reaffirmed the teaching of the encyclical as well as traditional teaching on premarital sexual intercourse, homosexuality and masturbation. In 1987 an *Instruction on Respect for Human Life in its Origin and on the Dignity of Procreation* from the same congregation disallowed *in vitro* fertilisation and embryo transfer techniques, again to the disappointment of some Catholic couples.

Beyond medico-moral problems, the galloping rate of change in the world of the twentieth century presented Christians with a myriad other challenges in daily living. Even in the previous century the effects of the Industrial Revolution had drastically altered the conditions of labour, often to the detriment of human dignity. With Pope Leo XIII's encyclical *Rerum Novarum* in 1891, the hierarchical magisterium began a series of interventions on these **social questions** that, necessarily, had to become more frequent; forty years passed before Pius XI covered the intervening period with *Quadragesimo Anno* (1931), then thirty years to John XXIII's *Mater et Magistra* (1961) and a shorter interval to John Paul II's *Laborem Exercens* (1981). All these papal statements

tried to take stock of the situation of contemporary industrial-
ised society and to spell out principles for Christian life
within it; at first addressed only to bishops, from John XXIII
onwards they were meant to help 'all men and women of
good will' theologise about the realities of their lives.

In the wake of decolonisation, the welfare of newly created
states in the Third World also pricked the conscience of
people in more prosperous, longer established nations. Poverty, hunger, oppression on a vast scale came to the forefront
of consciousness with the spread of visual communication
particularly. These economic and social questions involved
political and philosophical considerations as well, especially
with the advance of Marxist communism. Theologians wres-
tled with the moral implications of **development and under-
development**, as we shall see further in Chapter 12. The
hierarchical magisterium responded, too, in its manner: the
popes took account of the issues in encyclicals like John
XXIII's *Pacem in Terris* (1963), Paul VI's remarkable statement
on development *Populorum Progressio* (1967), and the letter
written to commemorate it twenty years later, *Sollicitudo Rei
Socialis* of John Paul II, who explained the purpose of such
social statements:

> The Church's social doctrine is not a 'third way' between liberal
> capitalism and Marxist collectivism, nor even a possible
> alternative to other solutions less radically opposed to one
> another: rather, it constitutes a category of its own. Nor is it an
> ideology, but rather the accurate formulation of the results of a
> careful reflection on the complex realities of human existence, in
> society and in the international order, in the light of faith and of
> the Church's tradition. Its main aim is to interpret these realities,
> determining their conformity with or divergence from the lines of
> the Gospel teaching on man and his vocation, a vocation which is
> at once earthly and transcendent; its aim is thus to guide Christian
> behaviour. It therefore belongs to the field, not of ideology, but of
> theology and particularly of moral theology.

> (*Sollicitudo Rei Socialis* 41)

National episcopal conferences also addressed these questions; John Paul II's address to the Latin American bishops at
Puebla in 1979 endorsed these principles (see Appendix for
text).

Amidst other such realities requiring (in the Pope's words)
interpretation, or theologising, for the guidance of Christian

59

behaviour in the modern world are issues like **enculturation**, ecology, war and peace. The Incarnation, of course, commits the Christian Church to a positive evaluation of people's culture, as I explain in Chapters 12 and 13; after the mistakes leading to the Eastern schism and the abortive attempts to Christianise the Orient, Western Christians have come to recognise legitimate cultural diversity, thanks also to biblical studies dealing with an enculturated yet inspired text. The relevance of this principle for evangelisation was explored by the 1974 Synod of Bishops on evangelisation in the modern world and clearly stated in its sequel, Paul VI's *Evangelii Nuntiandi*. Theology, as we shall see, takes various enculturated forms today. Theology, if not the hierarchical magisterium so much to date, is also sharing our contemporary **concern for the environment** and the future of our eco-system; creation theology, tapping into sapiential and Pauline insights in the Bible, is suggesting how we should treat responsibly the world given us by the Creator, who saw 'it was very good' and should remain so.

So the **rate of change** in modern society is posing a greater number of moral questions to the Christian community for settlement in the light of their foundational experiences. Fortunately, improved learning and technology allow updating of biblical and other traditions as well as the natural sciences, and so the community's moral teaching should also be able to keep pace. These developments together with a greater accent on freedom and responsibility should help the individual believer/theologian in moral decision-making.

Some relevant reading

Fuchs, J., *Human Values and Christian Morality*, Gill and Macmillan, Dublin, 1970.

Häring, B., *Free and Faithful in Christ*, 3 volumes, St Paul, Sydney, 1978–81.

Lewis, B., 'Approaches to morality in the Church today', *Word in Life* 32 (1984, no. 4) 17–19.

O'Connell, T. F., *Principles for a Christian Morality*, Seabury, New York, 1978.

Pope Paul VI, *The Regulation of Birth* (*Humanae Vitae*), Rome, 1968.

Vatican II, *Declaration on Christian Freedom*, Rome, 1965.

Exercises in theology

(1) Read Paul's letter to the Galatians, and note how he fumes against those who shackle Christian freedom by imposing Jewish restrictions on them — yet he also speaks of the law of Christ. Can you see how he upholds both freedom and law? Is there a recipe here for Christian morality?

(2) How competent do you feel about moral decision-making? How in touch are you with current teaching of the magisterium, relevant developments in biblical studies and moral theology? Describe the way in which you would form your conscience on a ticklish moral issue in an area of bioethics, modern warfare, social justice.

(3) Biblical studies have shown how inadequate is a 'Ten Commandments' approach to moral theology and moral education. What model of morality do you adopt in your thinking and teaching?

(4) List the areas of moral living where Catholics are looking for guidance today. Is help available in any of these areas from the hierarchical magisterium or theology, to the best of your knowledge?

11

Mistaking

the form for

the experience:

Fundamentalism

The faith of the Christian community (as of any community or individual) rests on experiences that are foundational and constitutive for that community. An **authentic faith** responds to God's action in those experiences as mediated accurately through the processes of tradition — biblical, liturgical, doctrinal, catechetical, and the lived tradition of the community. Hence the important role of theology in constantly subjecting transmissional processes to review lest faith be false; hence also Anselm's notion of theology as faith seeking understanding, and Augustine's statement of the close relationship between these two: 'Seek understanding with a view to faith. Have faith with a view to understanding.'

Christian history has, in fact, seen instances of inadequate or **misguided response** to foundational experiences through faulty or insufficient effort to relate faith and understanding. The Reformers castigated inadequacies of a certain type, while perhaps falling victim to a different theological aberration. The honest efforts at clarification by biblical critics over the last century did not always lead the simple faithful to an informed faith; many, disturbed also by political and economic upheaval, despaired of reaching any understanding and abandoned their faith for agnosticism — for them God, if not dead, was unattainable. Old 'certainties', of doctrine or scripture, were shown to be no longer certain: why keep treading the painful path towards an educated faith?

An alternative response in the face of upsetting change and review, a response equally self-defeating and intellectually lazy, has been to cling fast to the old 'certainties' and ignore the call to adaptation, *aggiornamento*. For Christians of this mindset 'it was good enough for Moses' (in the words of the song associated with the US 'Monkey Trial' of evolutionary theory dramatised in the film *Inherit the Wind*). The form in which the foundational experiences were 'always' transmitted is the form in which they will be received; in fact, the world is as it always has been. Stress falls on the *status quo*, not on the features of change and development discerned by sociologists as characteristic of our times. In the title of an important work by US evangelicals early this century, it is **The Fundamentals** that are important, not the changing way in which they are passed from age to age.

Hence the response of religious fundamentalism to the incarnate (and therefore enculturated, historically conditioned) Word: it is an attitude that is equally extreme as agnosticism, not simply conservative but **anti-intellectual** and lazy, **rationalistic** because opting for a principle of unchanging permanence in place of the revealed Christian principle of Incarnation, preferring to Anselm's dictum a 'faith insisting on permanence and certainty' instead of a continuing search for greater clarification. It is an attitude that affects politics, economics, social theory and education ('back to basics') as well as religion; though associated with the US south in particular, it is **world-wide** in its occurrence because its characteristics appeal to people everywhere who shun the relativity of human history and existence — from Catholicism in this country to Iranian Islam.

Fundamentalism is opposed to theology, as to any science that questions the adequacy of our knowledge of reality. Many of the movement's publications (to judge from the catalogues of publishing houses such as Garland Publishing, Inc., New York) assail the twin evils of **evolutionary theory** and **biblical criticism** because both discourage a superficial acceptance of traditional accounts of history. **Biblical fundamentalism** is its best-known branch; in brief, it reveals an unwillingness to accept the humanity of the incarnate Word, just as in the early Church difficulties surfaced first in regard to the humanity of Jesus. It is impatient of efforts of biblical criticism to highlight the historical conditioning of biblical texts and to provide evidence of the plurality and diversity of human authors and viewpoints in these texts. All types of biblical material are viewed similarly, so that apocalyptic (Daniel and Revelation being favourite texts) is treated as factual as Acts, for example. Inerrancy is the prime characteristic of biblical texts, as though Jesus' freedom from physical defect is more significant than his saving mission; the search for this **inerrancy**, ignoring the refinements of biblical criticism, leads fundamentalists into absurdities and distracts them from the saving purpose of the Word. They ignore the teaching of Pius XII in *Divino Afflante Spiritu* (1943), the Pontifical Biblical Commission's *Instruction on the Gospels* (1964), and Vatican II's *Constitution on Divine Revelation* (1965), not to mention the widely held positions of biblical scholars appearing consistently in prestigious journals over many decades.

Naturally, a fundamentalist attitude carries over into matters of **doctrine** and devotional practice. Because fundamentalists have a basic hermeneutical problem (i.e. a problem of interpreting texts, as in their treatment of biblical apocalyptic as history), they likewise apply Church statements indiscriminately, ignoring their relativity and historical conditioning; papal and Council documents are quoted out of context. In 1973 the Congregation for the Doctrine of Faith, itself not notorious for avant-garde pronouncements, rebuked this undiscriminating, uncritical tendency:

> Difficulties arise from the historical condition that affects the expression of revelation. With regard to this historical condition, it must first be observed that the meaning of the pronouncements of faith depends partly upon the expressive power of the language used at a certain point in time and in particular circumstances. Moreover, it sometimes happens that some dogmatic truth is first expressed incompletely (but not falsely), and at a later date, when considered in a broader context of faith or human knowledge, it receives a fuller and more perfect expression. In addition, when the Church makes new pronouncements, she intends to confirm or clarify what is in some way contained in Sacred Scripture or in previous expressions of Tradition; but at the same time she usually has the intention of solving certain questions or removing certain errors. All these things have to be taken into account in order that these pronouncements may be properly interpreted. Finally, even though the truths which the Church intends to teach through her dogmatic formulas are distinct from the changeable

conceptions of a given epoch and can be expressed without them, nevertheless it can sometimes happen that these truths may be enunciated by the Sacred Magisterium in terms that bear traces of such conceptions.

(*Mysterium Ecclesiae*)

As we have had occasion to note before, Catholic piety has not always found expression in **devotional practices** in keeping with a developing Church teaching, and these have required renewal through directives of the magisterium. Attachment to the person of Christ and his mother, laudable in itself and expressed in a variety of devotions that bespeak different theological tendencies, has at times settled for forms that are inadequate. The search for relics of Jesus' life and the saints in the Middle Ages, the veneration of miraculous shrines and images even today (cf. the Shroud of Turin) has not always been balanced by equal attention to the Word of God in the Bible; people travel long distances on the word of an apparition of the Mother of God without ever going to the trouble of reading an updated statement of Church teaching on her. There can be a fundamentalist tendency here to bypass the normal incarnational means to finding God in faith, such as the liturgy, Church teaching and theological scholarship. The charismatic movement, too, runs this risk: Scripture texts in particular can be selected and interpreted in a way foreign to biblical criticism. Beyond the Catholic community Pentecostalist excesses have come in for justified skepticism.

Writers on fundamentalism highlight the pastoral problem the movement poses for the Catholic community. There is no doubt that the gains made by theological scholarship in areas such as the interpretation of Scripture have not always reached the 'simple faithful'; educational resources are seldom directed to **continuing growth in faith** of adults. Many people have found a kind of satisfaction in fundamentalist groups that they have not experienced in the Catholic community. Inadequately educated adults are vulnerable to fundamentalist sects, and young people as well. Opportunities for 'doing theology' need to be more widespread so that believers may be brought more authentically into touch with the Christian mysteries.

Some relevant reading

Barr, J., *Fundamentalism*, SCM Press, London, 1978.

Boys, M., 'Fundamentalism', PACE 11 (1981).

Brown, R. E., *Biblical Exegesis and Church Doctrine*, Paulist, New York, 1985.

Hill, C., *Appreciating the Scriptures*, ACTS, Melbourne, 1986.

LaVerdiere, E., 'Fundamentalism', *The Bible Today* 21 (1983) 5–11.

McBrien, R., 'Teaching Catholicism today: the challenge of Fundamentalism', PACE 16 (1986).

Pope Pius XII, *Divino Afflante Spiritu* (on biblical studies), Rome, 1943.

Exercises in theology

(1) We all know people who lament 'changes in the Church', who regret the happening of Vatican II, who say they would like the old ways back, even the Latin Mass. Try to analyse precisely what lies behind these complaints (nostalgia, ignorance, laziness, malice, disillusionment, . . .). What can be done — by us, by them, by the community generally — to dispel this attitude?

(2) Examine a copy of your local Catholic newspaper for its success in bringing readers to a more enlightened appreciation of their beliefs, and also for any fundamentalist views by contributors or correspondents.

(3) Suppose you are entrusted with the planning of a program of adult education in your parish/region. Outline the areas of religious development in which Catholic adults most need help to offset fundamentalist attitudes.

(4) Do you think Catholic devotional life has kept pace with a developed theological understanding of the faith? Nominate several Catholic devotional practices (e.g. the rosary, the Way of the Cross), and suggest the degree of support they find in the Scriptures, liturgical practice, current Church teaching.

12

Receiving

the tradition in

diverse situations:

Third World theology

The Incarnation is at the heart of the Christian experience, even if we have seen a (regrettable?) movement in Christian thinking from Pauline and Gospel insistence on the Paschal Mystery of Jesus to his conception and birth in the statements of the early Councils –– something obviously not basic to the New Testament message. For the Christian, revelation and salvation are incarnated in the man Jesus, a Palestinian Jew of the first century. We have seen the early community struggling to accept the **implications of Incarnation**; John and Ignatius within a century of Jesus' death had to insist on the fact of Incarnation, on the reality of Jesus' humanity against dualistic heresies (like Gnosticism) that looked askance at divine acceptance of the human condition.

Later ages, too, resisted the full acceptance of the marvellous divine *koinōnia*, sharing, self-communication, that Jesus represents (expressed so eloquently, as we saw, by Chrysostom and other Greek Fathers). Difficulties with Jesus' humanity often lead to correlative difficulties with acceptance of that other, scriptural Incarnation, where the Word is present 'in human language to become like human discourse' (*Dogmatic Constitution on Divine Revelation* 13). The findings of biblical criticism have proved a scandal for those unwilling to accept the literary and **cultural conditioning** of the divine Word in the Bible (see Chapter 8). Fundamentalists cannot concede that truth appears in different ways according to the different forms and circumstances of Church statements and biblical types (see Chapter 11).

Just as God's revelation and salvation come to us in this incarnational, human, conditioned way, so our response to God's action in Jesus is likewise affected by our human situation. The various traditions by which the experience of Jesus is transmitted to later generations are affected by similar **incarnational factors** as he is — factors of time, place, culture, even sex. The variety of biblical composition, the differences between Eastern and Western liturgies, the different philosophical underpinning of various Church statements — all reflect the initial divine acceptance of the world and humanity in the man Jesus. Christians' response in faith to Jesus takes a variety of forms because Christians live in a variety of times, places, cultures. The Incarnation requires it.

Just as there have been those reluctant to accept historical and cultural conditioning in Jesus, so there are those who envisage only one unvariegated expression of faith by all Christians. The Church learnt to its cost that evangelisation of Asia could not succeed if one, European, Roman model of church and worship was imposed on orientals; **enculturation** is only now being accepted as a principle of Church life, too late to correct that earlier mistake. And yet the whole centre of gravity of Christianity has shifted from Europe to the Third World continents of Africa and South America. Whereas at the beginning of this century Europe and North America accounted for 85 per cent of all Christians, by the end of the century it has been calculated (e.g. by Walbert Bühlmann) that this figure will fall to 42 per cent, leaving 58 per cent of Christians in the 'Third Church' (in his words). In the two decades from 1952 to 1972 the number of African Catholics tripled from 12.5 million to 36 million; and whereas the number of priests plummeted in European countries in those years, they soared from 1400 to 4200 in Africa, where the seminaries are bulging.

European Christianity has come to admit that its Third World counterpart might worship in forms different from what was once regarded narrowly as 'traditional'. African rhythms have replaced the Gregorian chant as appropriate liturgical expression in that continent. The dire poverty of South American favelas produces artistic representations of

the crucified Christ that are much more tortured and ex-
cruciating than are those of the relatively comfortable 'Old
Masters'; being a Christian there produces a different notion
of suffering and oppression. So it is not surprising — though
Europe was slow to accept it — that believers should reflect
on their faith in word and writing in a **different style of
theology** in the Third World. Africa has produced its own
African theology, South East Asia its Water Buffalo theology,
an Australian theologian speaks of Boomerang theology, and
in South America there developed Liberation theology (just
as that continent produced a distinct educational theory in
Freire's 'pedagogy of the oppressed').

What Jesus means to Christian women and men — and the
New Testament offers a **range of figures**, including redemp-
tion, salvation, new creation, reconciliation, atonement —
varies according to the viewpoint of the believer. In an
oppressed situation, economically, politically, socially, such
as that of South America, Jesus comes as a **liberator**, as he
describes himself in the Gospel of the oppressed:

> He opened the book and found the place where it was written,
>   'The Spirit of the Lord is upon me,
>   because he has anointed me to preach the good news to the
>   poor.
>   He has sent me to proclaim release to the captives
>   and recovering sight to the blind,
>   to set at liberty those who are oppressed,
>   to proclaim the acceptable year of the Lord.' (Is 16)
> And he closed the book, and gave it back to the attendant, and sat
> down; and the eyes of all in the synagogue were fixed on him.
> And he began to say to them, 'Today this scripture has been
> fulfilled in your hearing.'
>
> (Luke 4:18–21)

With this and further scriptural encouragement **liberation
theologians** apply Christian beliefs to the oppressed situation
of believers, from which Christ comes to deliver them:

> In the liberation approach sin is not considered as an individual,
> private, or merely interior reality — asserted just enough to
> necessitate a 'spiritual' redemption which does not challenge the
> order in which we live. Sin is regarded as a social, historical fact,
> the absence of brotherhood and love in relationships among
> people, the breach of friendship with God and other people, and

therefore an interior, personal fracture . . . Sin is evident in oppressive structures, in the exploitation of man by man, in the domination and slavery of peoples, races, and social classes. Sin appears, therefore, as the fundamental alienation, the root of a situation of injustice and exploitation . . .

This radical liberation is the gift which Christ offers us. By his death and resurrection he redeems human beings from sin and all its consequences, as has been well said in a text we quote again: 'It is the same God who, in the fulness of time, sends his Son in the flesh, so that he might come to liberate all men from *all* slavery to which sin has subjected them: hunger, misery, oppression, and ignorance — in a word, that injustice and hatred which have their origin in human selfishness' (Latin American Bishops at Medellin).

(Gutierrez, 1974, pp. 175–6)

For liberation theologians like Gustavo Gutierrez, Leonardo Boff, Juan Luis Segundo, the Christian message must take account of the social, economic and political situation of the believer — just as Jesus did. Since that situation is one of oppression and deprivation, the Christian message will be one of liberation — just as Jesus' was. No **sanctification** without first **humanisation**. For some theologians and authorities from the First and Second Worlds, accustomed to a less conditioned theology for a less deprived people, such incarnational theology came as a shock — as did the man Jesus to some of his contemporaries. This response to liberation theology occurred despite Pope Paul VI's lengthy treatment of liberation in his 1975 apostolic exhortation *Evangelii Nuntiandi* (29–39) and John Paul II's address to the South American bishops at Puebla in 1979 (see Appendix for text).

So in 1984 the Sacred Congregation for the Doctrine of the Faith published an *Instruction on Certain Aspects of the Theology of Liberation*, presenting a very negative view, based on an inadequate commentary on the New Testament (not even citing that key Lucan passage), neglecting those key papal teachings, seeing the object of liberation as the conversion of the oppressor rather than alleviation of the condition of the oppressed. But following discussion between the Brazilian bishops and Pope John Paul, the same congregation two years later produced an *Instruction on Christian Freedom and Liberation* allowing the validity of a theology which does not ignore the condition of the believer (though still in a guarded way, and still strangely ignoring the Gospel of the oppressed):

70

A theological reflection developed from a particular experience can constitute a very positive contribution, inasmuch as it makes possible a highlighting of aspects of the Word of God, the richness of which had not yet been fully grasped. But in order that this reflection may be truly a reading of the Scripture and not a projection on to the Word of God of a meaning which it does not contain, the theologian will be careful to interpret the experience from which he begins in the light of the experience of the Church herself. This experience of the Church shines with a singular brightness and in all its purity in the lives of saints. It pertains to the pastors of the Church, in communion with the Successor of Peter, to discern its authenticity.   (70)

In future, hopefully, there will be no doubts of the legitimacy of such theologies — Liberation, Black, Red, African, Boomerang, Water Buffalo or others. Likewise, the particular theological perspective of women is calling for recognition in the writings of **feminist theologians** like Rosemary Ruether and Elizabeth Schüssler Fiorenza. All Christians respond in faith to the same foundational experiences; but the form of their response to these experiences, as also to the traditions that transmit them, will vary if human beings are involved.

Some relevant reading

Bühlmann, W., *The Coming of the Third Church*, St Paul, Slough, 1976.

Freire, P., *Pedagogy of the Oppressed*, Penguin, Harmondsworth, 1972.

Goosen, G., 'Boomerang theology on materialism', *Compass Theology Review* 17 (1984 Summer) 16–26.

Gutierrez, G., *A Theology of Liberation*, SCM press, London, 1974.

Keller, J., 'Women as religious educators', *Word in Life* 35 (1987 August) 5–13.

Lane, D., *Foundations for a Social Theology*, Gill and Macmillan, Dublin, 1984.

Pope Paul VI, *On the Development of Peoples* (*Progressio Populorum*), Rome, 1967.

——, *Evangelisation in the Modern World* (*Evangelii Nuntiandi*), Rome, 1975.

Exercises in theology

(1) Do you think we the Church do enough to accommodate the Christian message to the condition of the believer? Consider things like children's Masses, attention to migrants' needs, sexism in Church language, communication in the Church, ... What other aspects of Church life should be affected by the principle of incarnation?

(2) Like most of the world's Catholics we live away from the original centres of Christendom; perhaps our climate, seasons, hemisphere are different. To what extent have we developed our own culture? Mention the distinctive features of this culture; then discuss how far this distinctiveness colours the way we live the faith and theologise about it in our country.

(3) How multicultural is our religious education? If we say our society is multicultural, does that lead to a recognition of diversity in our student body in racial attitudes, religious background, style of celebration, etc.? Describe your provision for multiculturalism in your religious education programming.

13

Theology,

faith,

religion,

religious education

This book is very much about **faith** — as any theological activity is about faith. There are surely many definitions of **theology**, but, in a nutshell, Anselm's eleventh century one-liner says it all: 'faith seeking understanding'. Karl Rahner, not known for one-liners, defines theology as 'the conscious and methodical explanation and explication of the divine revelation received and grasped in faith'. Both theologians, centuries apart, see theology beginning with faith, whatever of the hypothetical possibility of the non-believing profes-sional 'theologian' making a living writing books on theology or the Bible (not the case with this book, let it be said!). **Religion**, too, is much about faith: it stems from faith and expresses in various forms a relationship born of faith, even if the forms are human and the faith gift divine.

Christian **religious education** is at least basically about faith, in its presuppositions and in some of its intentions and outcomes. This would apply to the various contexts and ages at which it takes place. It can be called faith education, even if its scope may be also to educate about religion and religions. In the history of Christianity, and before it in Judaism, growth in faith was seen related to education and growth in understanding. We have seen Augustine formulating the relationship: 'Seek understanding with a view to faith; have faith with a view to understanding'. And we have examined periods of Christian history, including our own, where an authentic faith response has been retarded through **inadequate education** in the traditions of Christianity. The Incarnation, which we have taken as paradigm both of Christian gift and Christian response, demands that human effort be made to nourish what has been received from God without that effort.

Faith (and therefore theology) is very much about **experience** — which is not to say it depends on feelings. We have looked at periods in history when preoccupation with system or attachment to form has kept the believer from tapping into those experiences of God's action (pre-eminently in Jesus) that prompted the faith of the initial believers and shaped the community. At every stage of Christian history, no matter how remote from the time of Jesus, faith has depended on **access to those experiences** — hence the importance in religious education of continuing that tradition. In the Bible, in the liturgy, in doctrinal and catechetical traditions, in the lived tradition of the community I meet Jesus and become associated with his Paschal Mystery, and my faith is nourished and authenticated. If I express a longing for religious experience of my own, for getting something out of the liturgy, for coming to know the Lord personally, I am looking for nothing more nor less than what brought Paul to faith and made a missioner of him. Faith is, in other words, about story: about **my story** and Jesus' story, about Paul's story and **the community's story**; like Paul, and Aquinas, and Luther, and Bultmann, I need to bring my story together with the community's story by experiencing Jesus myself, or my faith withers. Paul met Jesus on the road to Damascus, but he had also to quiz Peter on the community's experience of him (*Galatians* 1:18). Yes, faith and theology (and religious education) are about experience.

Faith is about **revelation**, as Rahner suggested above. The experience of God we receive, directly or dependently, brings us a share in God's self-communication — *koinōnia* in the language of the New Testament. We share in God's own life and what else he has to communicate to us of himself. Such revelation comes to us definitively in Jesus — hence the importance of those traditions that pass that revelatory experience on to us (as we pass it on in religious education). Reading the biblical accounts of God's actions and involving ourselves in the liturgy should also prove revelatory experiences for us. We are often brought to see God's purposes by the people we meet and the things that happen to us in life's journey, and our faith response is stimulated.

Faith is not about **forms**. Religion, rather, is about forms; faith declares itself in a variety of religious expression, as the Incarnation again requires. Likewise, tradition of the foundational experience involves oral and written records, forms of word in definition, rituals of celebration. But a living faith can outgrow the forms to search for better ones, and attachment to an outmoded, inadequate form can be stifling for faith; prophets from Isaiah onwards have criticised religion for this. The Incarnation teaches us that **change and development** are characteristic of Christian living as of all life; a fundamentalist rejection of new formulas or fresh vision results only in a deadening of faith. Religious education, like the Church generally, must always be searching for contemporary means of articulating the mystery — the vast sacred reality that is the mystery (not the 'puzzle') of Christ.

Likewise, faith is not unaffected by **conditions**, **cultures**, **times** — like the man Jesus himself. James in the New Testament ('that epistle of straw', as Luther said in one of his less happy scriptural comments) knew there is little faith education in telling the starving man to 'offer it up' and look towards eternity — something the Church once had a name for. Inhuman conditions are not fertile soil for faith development or any other human development; **humanisation**, liberation was therefore very much Jesus' mission. Matteo Ricci might have been able to be countermanded in his recipe for the conversion of China by the Church of the seventeenth century, but **enculturation** is now accepted as a principle of faith education throughout the Church, if not yet everywhere adopted. A vital Australian Church is likewise committed to a multicultural religious education, aware of cultural groups and oppressed minorities.

We have seen the role of **tradition** in forming faith. A mature faith is the result of keeping in touch with all the traditions of the community of faith, though we have had difficulty down through the ages keeping them all fresh and vital. Only the most recent Council has told Catholics: 'From the table of both the Word of God and the Body of Christ the Church unceasingly receives and offers the bread of life, especially in the sacred liturgy' (*Dogmatic Constitution on Divine Revelation* 21). Keeping in touch with the Church's biblical, liturgical, doctrinal traditions is a demanding **task for religious educators**, as for all believers, but only in that direction lies authentic, mature faith.

Such faith development is clearly **a lifelong task**. Children, of course, are theologising once they begin trying to make sense of what they believe or the community believes, but the questions become more profound and wide-ranging as we grow older in a rapidly changing world. Formation of conscience for responsible use of Christian freedom is also a lengthy process, yet we require it for appreciation of the Christian moral tradition. The Incarnation again suggests that this maturing will not take place without sustained, conscious effort, though the community has not always applied this effort to the benefit of its members after school age. 'Doing theology' is something they need help with throughout life — hence the writing of this little book.

Some relevant reading

Dulles, A., *Models of Revelation*, Doubleday, New York, 1982.

Gascoigne, R., 'The relationship of faith and knowledge', *Word in Life* 35 (1987 February) 8–12.

Miller, D. E., *Story and Context. An Introduction to Christian Education*, Abingdon, Nashville, 1987.

National Catholic Education Commission, *Towards Adult Faith*, NCEC, Melbourne, 1983.

Thornhill, J., 'Handing on the faith', *Word in Life* 35 (1987 May) 5–9.

Vatican II, *Dogmatic Constitution on Divine Revelation*, Rome, 1965.

Exercises in theology

(1) Could you say your study of theology has strengthened your faith, in the way St Augustine saw the relationship of faith and theology? Conversely, do you see how ignorance of theology could retard your faith development? Is the same true of sound religious education and faith, in your experience?

(2) Like Paul, we all have our own spiritual journey, with its peaks and troughs. Trace your own journey, touching on highlights at which an insight into God's purposes has broken through for you. Does it help to place your journey alongside the faith community's, from Paschal Mystery to parousia?

(3) How well equipped are you as an agent of Christian tradition? How well do you know Christianity's biblical tradition? Are you an active participant in its liturgical tradition? Can your students turn to you for an updated statement of Catholic doctrinal tradition? If not, what are you doing about it?

14

Sources and resources

for the task of theology

Theology, as we have seen, endeavours to bring some understanding to faith experiences — the community's and our own. Our participation in the community's foundational experiences is not direct; we depend on their transmission by others. We turn, therefore, to the traditional forms assembled by the community over the ages. For some account of that **historical development** we might look at works such as

Bettenson, H., *Documents of the Christian Church*, (2nd edn), Oxford University Press, New York, 1967.
Deiss, L., *Springtime of the Liturgy*, Liturgical Press, Collegeville, 1979.
Grant, R. and Tracy, D., *A Short History of the Interpretation of the Bible*, Fortress, Philadelphia, 1984.
Kelly, J. N. D., *Early Christian Creeds*, (3rd edn), Longman, London, 1972.
___, *Early Christian Doctrines*, (5th edn), Harper and Row, New York, 1978.
Shelly, B., *Church History in Plain Language*, Word Books, Waco, 1982.

Of all the traditions passing on to us Christianity's foundational experiences, **the biblical record** has a particular value; we reverence it as the Word of God. To be able to read it (without questioning its bona fides or puzzling over its meaning) we need a sound modern **translation** of the Bible. There are many of these, differing somewhat on the score of the kind of readership intended. For a discussion of the differences involved that may affect our choice, see W. A. Hutchinson, 'Selecting a Bible: which translation?' *The Living Light* 17 (1980) 350–6. Check that your Bible is a Catholic one in the sense that it contains the deuterocanonical books of the Old Testament (not included in some editions of the Bible).

Once we are sure that we have a reliable translation, various avenues of study open up which have been well travelled by scholars before us. Charting these various avenues will be helped by some general **bibliography**, like that of J. A. Fitzmyer, *An Introductory Bibliography for the Study of Scripture*, rev. edn, Biblical Institute, Rome, 1981. To deal with particular books of the Bible we will need to refer to those general treatments, comprehensive rather than elementary, yet bearing the misleading title of '**Introduction**'. For the Old Testament we can try B. S. Childs, *Introduction to the Old Testament as Scripture*, SCM Press, London, 1979, or the simpler one by B. W. Anderson, *The Living World of the Old Testament (Understanding the Old Testament* in the USA), 3rd edn, Longman, London, 1978. For the New Testament the standard work is W. G. Kümmell *Introduction to the New Testament*, 17th edn, SCM Press, London, 1975 (now in its 19th German edition). A Catholic alternative is R. F. Collins, *Introduction to the New Testament*, Doubleday, New York, 1983. There is a range of **commentaries** on the individual books, from the scholarly *Anchor Bible* series to the simpler Catholic ones, *Old Testament Message* and *New Testament Message*.

Sometimes we may be satisfied to read the work of (other) scholars of the Bible; in this case we may want to consult recent **journal articles** on some biblical topic, and abstracts of all such articles occur in *Old Testament Abstracts* and *New Testament Abstracts* published several times a year. Our own research on the text of the Bible (if only in translation from the Hebrew or Greek originals) will be assisted by lexical tools such as a **concordance** (which simply lists all the occurrences in the Bible of a term like 'faith') or a **theological dictionary** of either testament, which goes a step further in discussing these occurrences; a **synopsis** is a book which lists parallel scriptural passages, say, in the Gospels. A plain **Bible dictionary** (as distinct from a **lexicon** of a biblical language) will give us information on a range of items referred to in the Bible; a **Bible atlas** will help us with geography and topography.

Whereas the Bible recounts the community's experiences, **the liturgy** has the advantage of bringing them to life in celebration — *anamnesis,* as the liturgy itself refers to this special way of remembering. So the best liturgical resource is a living liturgical celebration. One may consult a **history** of the Church's forms down the centuries, like that of Deiss or J. Martos, *Doors to the Sacred,* SCM Press, London, 1981, to see the extent to which liturgical tradition of the Christian mystery has remained authentic. There are more **general treatments** of the nature of Christian liturgy available, like C. Jones *et al.* (eds), *The Study of Liturgy,* SPCK, London, 1978, or J. G. Davies (ed.), *A Dictionary of Liturgy and Worship,* 2nd edn, SCM Press, London, 1987, or **particular treatment** of the sacraments in a series like M. Hellwig (ed.), *Message of the Sacraments,* Michael Glazier, Wilmington. For the Catholic community's liturgy an important resource is the teaching of **the magisterium,** documented in M. Simcoe (ed.), *The Liturgy Documents: A Parish Resource,* 2nd edn, Liturgy Training Publications, Chicago, 1985, or a similar collection by the International Commission on English in the Liturgy, *Documents on the Liturgy 1963–1979: Conciliar, Papal and Curial Texts,* Liturgical Press, Collegeville, 1982. More periodic discussion and research can be found in **journals** like the US *Worship* or the Australian *Liturgy News.*

The Church's **doctrinal tradition** is not so readily arrived at, even from a simply Western perspective. As I pointed out in Chapter 11 on Fundamentalism, **printed formulas** from Rome or Trent, from a pope or bishop or Council at one time or another do not line up equally as statement of the Catholic community's belief — just as we have to be discerning in interpreting different forms of biblical expression, such as poetry or apocalyptic. There are collections of these formulas to be had; for those with a classical background a quasi-official handbook (*Enchiridion*) of Church statements collected by two Germans, Denzinger and Schönmetzer (Herder, Freiburg), had been so popular before Vatican II that it reached thirty-two editions until that Council's bulky documents effectively put it out of business. Collections of Church teaching before Vatican II (to be read with the above caveat) include K. Rahner (ed.), *The Teaching of the Catholic Church,* Mercier, Cork, 1966, and J. Neuner and J. Dupuis (eds), *The Christian Faith in the Doctrinal Documents of the Catholic Church,* 2nd edn, Mercier, Cork, 1983. Since the Council a vast six-volume encyclopedia, *Sacramentum Mundi,* appeared (ed.

K. Rahner, Herder, New York, 1968), handily digested in K. Rahner (ed.), *Encyclopedia of Theology. The Concise Sacramentum Mundi*, Burns and Oates, London 1975; a one-man attempt is R. McBrien *Catholicism*, Dove Communications, Melbourne, 1981.

There is place for **theological dictionaries** that throw light on theological notions and movements, like *The Westminster Dictionary of Christian Theology*, eds A. Richardson and J. Bowden, Westminster Press, Philadelphia, 1983, and for those that provide also an **historical perspective**, eminently *The Oxford Dictionary of the Christian Church*, 2nd edn, eds F. Cross and E. Livingstone, Oxford University Press, London, 1974.

Of course, we could assemble our own text by reading (after the Bible) **the Fathers of the Church** over six centuries in the modern patristic series, *The Fathers of the Church* (Catholic University of America Press, Washington) and *Ancient Christian Writers* (Paulist, New York). For recent theological investigation (beyond our own) in the area of doctrine we need to refer to some of a vast range of **journals**: *Theological Studies* and *Concilium* would be more sophisticated than the Australian *Compass Theology Review* and *Australasian Catholic Record*.

So we are not short of equipment for **our task as theologians**. It is, in fact, a task, a responsibility for the believer. For St Thomas, with his Aristotelian categories, theology was a habit, to be developed by practice, even if he could also describe it in more exalted terms as 'a certain participation in God's own knowledge of himself' (*Summa Theologiae*, Ia, q. 1, a. 3) and St Augustine could speak of us as ravished by desire for following up this truth (*De Trinitate*). It lies within our reach, therefore, this possibility of following the prompting of our faith to attain the object of our hope in love. After theology, said the great Thomistic commentator Cajetan, only the beatific vision.

APPENDIX

Apostles Creed

The present text of this creed is not known to be older than the sixth century; there was then a 'tradition' that each article had been composed by one of the Apostles. But it resembles Roman creeds going back to about AD 200, and all its articles are found in even earlier formulas of faith.

I believe in God, the Father Almighty,
    Creator of heaven and earth,
and in Jesus Christ, his only Son, our Lord,
who was conceived by the Holy Ghost,
    born of the Virgin Mary;
suffered under Pontius Pilate,
    was crucified, dead, and buried;
He descended into hell;
    the third day he rose again from the dead;
He ascended into heaven,
    is seated at the right hand of God, the Father
    Almighty;
thence he shall come to judge the living and the dead.
I believe in the Holy Ghost,
the holy catholic Church,
the Communion of Saints,
the forgiveness of sins,
the resurrection of the body,
and life everlasting. Amen.

Nicene–Constantinopolitan Creed

Often called the Nicene Creed, it differs from the creed produced at Nicea in AD 325 and was in fact composed at the First Council of Constantinople in AD 381, though said mistakenly to be an amplification of the earlier creed — hence its name. It was introduced into the Mass in the West from the sixth century with the addition of the word *Filioque* ('and from the Son') in the article about the procession of the Holy Spirit, which gave great offence in the East for many centuries.

We believe in one God,
   the Father, the Almighty,
   maker of heaven and earth,
   of all that is, seen and unseen.
We believe in one Lord, Jesus Christ,
   the only Son of God,
   eternally begotten of the Father,
   God from God, Light from Light
   true God from true God,
   begotten, not made,
   of one Being with the Father.
   Through him all things were made.
For us men and for our salvation
   he came down from heaven:
   by the power of the Holy Spirit
he became incarnate from the Virgin Mary, and was
   made man.
   For our sake he was crucified under Pontius Pilate;
   he suffered death and was buried.
   On the third day he rose again
      in accordance with the Scriptures;
   he ascended into heaven
      and is seated at the right hand of the Father.
He will come again in glory to judge the living and
   the dead,
   and his kingdom will have no end.
We believe in the Holy Spirit, the Lord, the giver of life,
   who proceeds from the Father and the Son.
   With the Father and the Son he is worshipped and
      glorified.
   He has spoken through the Prophets.
   We believe in one holy catholic and apostolic Church.
   We acknowledge one baptism for the forgiveness of sins.
   We look for the resurrection of the dead,
      and the life of the world to come.
         Amen.

Pontifical Biblical Commission:
Instruction on the Historical Truth of the Gospels

Set up in 1902 by Pope Leo XIII with a membership of the world's best Catholic scholars, the Commission under Pius X during the Modernist crisis adopted a very cautionary, even repressive, role. Meantime biblical scholars were applying historical criticism to the New Testament. So it came as great encouragement to Catholic scholars that in 1964 the Commission, after a long silence, produced this positive endorsement of the findings of biblical criticism.

2. In order to determine correctly the trustworthiness of what is transmitted in the Gospels, the interpreter must take careful note of the three stages of tradition by which the teaching and the life of Jesus have come down to us.

Christ our Lord attached to Himself certain chosen disciples who had followed Him from the beginning, who had seen His works and had heard His words, and thus were qualified to become witnesses of His life and teaching. Our Lord, when expounding His teaching by word of mouth, observed the methods of reasoning and of exposition which were in common use at the time; in this way He accommodated Himself to the mentality of His hearers, and ensured that His teachings would be deeply impressed on their minds and would be easily retained in memory by His disciples. These latter grasped correctly the idea that the miracles and other events of the life of Jesus were things purposely performed or arranged by Him in such a way that men would thereby be led to believe in Christ and to accept by faith the doctrine of salvation.

The Apostles, bearing testimony of Jesus, proclaimed first and foremost the death and resurrection of the Lord, faithfully recounting His life and words and, as regards the manner of their preaching, taking into account the circumstances of their hearers. After Jesus had risen from the dead, and when His divinity was clearly perceived, the faith of the disciples, far from blotting out the remembrance of the events that had happened, rather consolidated it, since their faith was based on what Jesus had done and taught. Nor was Jesus transformed into a 'mythical' personage, and His teaching distorted, by reason of the worship which the disciples now paid Him, revering Him as Lord and Son of God. Yet it need not be denied that the Apostles, when handing on to their hearers the things which in actual fact the Lord had said and done, did so in the light of that fuller understanding which they enjoyed as a result of being schooled by the glorious things accomplished in Christ, and of being illumined by the Spirit of Truth. Thus it came about that, just as Jesus Himself after His resurrection had 'interpreted to them' both the words of the Old Testament and the words which He Himself had spoken, so now they in their turn interpreted His words and deeds according to the needs of their hearers. 'Devoting (themselves) to the ministry of the word,' they made use, as they preached, of such various forms of speech as were adopted to their own purposes and to the mentality of their hearers; for it was 'to Greek and barbarian, to learned and simple,' that they had a duty to discharge. These varied ways of speaking which the heralds of Christ made use of in proclaiming Him must be distinguished one from the other and carefully appraised: catecheses, narratives, testimonies, hymns, doxologies, prayers and any other such literary forms as were customarily employed in Sacred Scripture and by people of that time.

The sacred authors, for the benefit of the churches, took this earliest body of instruction, which had been handed on orally at first and then in writing — for many soon set their hands to 'drawing up a narrative' of matters concerning the Lord Jesus — and set it down in the four Gospels. In doing this each of them followed a method suitable to the special purpose which he had in view. They selected certain things out of the many which had been handed on; some they synthesized, some they explained with an eye to the situation of the churches, painstakingly using every means of bringing home to their readers the solid truth of the things in which they had been instructed. For, out of the material which they had received, the sacred authors selected especially those items which were adapted to the varied circumstances of the faithful as well as to the end which they themselves wished to attain; these they recounted in a manner consonant with those circumstances and with that end. And since the meaning of a statement depends, amongst other things, on the place which it has in a given sequence, the Evangelists, in handing on the words or the deeds of our Savior, explained them for the advantage of their readers by respectively setting them, one Evangelist in one context, another in another. For this reason the exegete must ask himself what the Evangelist intended by recounting a saying or a fact in a certain way, or by placing it in a certain context. For the truth of the narrative is not affected in the slightest by the fact that the Evangelists report the sayings or the doings of our Lord in a different order, and that they use different words to express what He said, not keeping to the very letter, but nevertheless preserving the sense . . .

Pope John Paul II at Puebla, January 1979

By the third quarter of the twentieth century, the Catholic population of Latin America constituted half the Church, most living in conditions of deprivation and oppression. A few months after his election the Pope travelled to Mexico to address the bishops of Latin America and recommend a pastoral approach that took account of these people's difficulties.

. . . From you, pastors, the faithful of your countries expect and demand above all a careful and zealous transmission of the truth concerning Jesus Christ. This truth is at the centre of evangelisation and constitutes its essential content: 'There is no true evangelisation if the name, the teaching, the life, the promises, the kingdom and the mystery of Jesus of Nazareth, the Son of God, are not proclaimed' (EN [Pope Paul VI's *Evangelii Nuntiandi*] 18) . . .

It is from a solid Christology that there must come light on so many doctrinal and pastoral themes and questions that you intend to study in these coming days . . .

There is no guarantee of serious and vigorous evangelising activity without a well-founded ecclesiology.

The first reason is that evangelisation is the essential mission, the distinctive vocation and the deepest identity of the Church, which has in turn been evangelised (EN 14–15; LG [Vatican II's *Lumen Gentium*] 5). She has been sent by the Lord and in her turn sends evangelisers to preach 'not their own selves or their personal ideas but a Gospel of which neither she nor they are the absolute masters and owners, to dispose of it as they wish' (EN 15).

A second reason is that 'evangelisation is for no one an individual and isolated act, it is one that is deeply ecclesial' (EN 60), which is not subject to the discretionary power of individualistic criteria and perspectives but to that of communion with the Church and her pastors . . .

The truth that we owe to man is, first and foremost, a truth about man. As witnesses of Jesus Christ we are heralds, spokesmen and servants of this truth. We cannot reduce it to the principles of a system of philosophy or to pure political activity. We cannot forget it or betray it.

Perhaps one of the most obvious weaknesses of present day civilisation lies in an inadequate view of man. Without doubt, our age is the one in which man has been most written of and spoken of, the age of the forms of humanism and the age of anthropocentrism. Nevertheless it is paradoxically also the age of man's deepest anxiety about his identity and his destiny, the age of man's abasement to previously unsuspected levels, the age of human values trampled on as never before . . .

Those familiar with the Church's history know that in all periods there have been admirable bishops deeply involved in advancing and valiantly defending the human dignity of those entrusted to them by the Lord. They have always been impelled to do so by their episcopal mission, because they considered human dignity a Gospel value that cannot be despised without greatly offending the Creator.

This dignity is infringed on the individual level when due regard is not had for values such as freedom, the right to profess one's religion, physical and mental integrity, the right to essential goods, to life . . . It is infringed on the social and political level when man cannot exercise his right of participation, or when he is subjected to unjust and unlawful coercion, or submitted to physical or mental torture, etc.

I am not unaware of how many questions are being posed in this sphere today in Latin America. As bishops, you cannot fail to concern yourselves with them. I know that you propose to carry out a serious reflection on the relationships and implications between evangelisation and human advancement or liberation, taking into consideration, in such a vast and important field, what is specific about the Church's presence.

Here is where we find, brought concretely into practice, the themes we have touched upon in speaking of the truth concerning Christ, the Church and man.

If the Church makes herself present in the defence of or in the advancement of man, she does so in line with her mission, which, although it is religious and not social or political, cannot fail to consider man in the entirety of his being . . .

Index

(Basic theological terms like *faith, religion, revelation, experience, tradition* occur repeatedly in the text and are not indexed here.)